THE POWER
TO PREDICT

THE POWER TO PREDICT

How Real-Time Businesses
Anticipate Customer Needs,
Create Opportunities,
and Beat the Competition

Vivek Ranadivé

McGraw-Hill

New York   Chicago   San Francisco   Lisbon   London   Madrid   Mexico City
Milan   New Delhi   San Juan   Seoul   Singapore   Sydney   Toronto

The McGraw·Hill Companies

1 2 3 4 5 6 7 8 9 0 DOC/DOC 0 9 8 7 6

ISBN 0-07-145014-9

This publication is designed to provide accurate and authoritative information in regard to the subject matter covered. It is sold with the understanding that the publisher is not engaged in rendering legal, accounting, or other professional service. If legal advice or other expert assistance is required, the services of a competent professional person should be sought.
>   —From a declaration of principles jointly adopted by a committee of
>   the American Bar Association and a committee of publishers.

McGraw-Hill books are available at special quantity discounts to use as premiums and sales promotions, or for use in corporate training programs. For more information, please write to the Director of Special Sales, McGraw-Hill Professional, Two Penn Plaza, New York, NY 10121-2298. Or contact your local bookstore.

This book is printed on recycled, acid-free paper containing a minimum of 50% recycled, de-inked fiber.

Library of Congress Cataloging-in-Publication Data

Ranadivé, Vivek

The power to predict: how real-time businesses anticipate customer needs, create opportunities, and beat the competition / By Vivek Ranadivé.— 1st ed.
    p. cm.
Includes bibliographical references and index.
ISBN 0-07-145014-9
    1. Real-time data processing—Management. 2. Business—Data processing—Management. 3. Selling. 4. Customer services. 5. Consumer satisfaction. I. Title.
    HF5548.3.R36 2006
658.7′03—dc22
                                                    2005034472

I would like to dedicate this book to my children, Aneel, Andre and Anjali, who are my pride and joy, and to my father, "The Captain," who taught me to never give up, and to my sister Smita, who has always been there for me.

Contents

FOREWORD

I MET VIVEK RANADIVÉ SOME years ago, not long after our companies started doing business together. In getting to know him better, I also found some interesting parallels between our mutual experiences as entrepreneurs.

Both of us built businesses around a simple concept that could be used to great effect in solving a complex problem. FedEx used the hub-and-spoke concept to solve the inefficiencies of point-to-point shipping whereas Vivek used the notion of a general integration software layer to solve the inefficiencies of point-to-point connections between the software applications that run most companies.

I believe Vivek has it right in thinking that the information that drives business today can be harnessed to allow a new level of foresight, especially when we are able to analyze that information in real time and detect meaningful patterns before they become problems or lost opportunities.

We at FedEx learned long ago that our business depends on real-time monitoring, performance measurement and rapid problem resolution. Today, virtually all businesses are driven by similar imperatives and need to know more about their operations more quickly. *The Power to Predict* talks about taking the next step by using a continuous information flow to literally "see around the corner." This concept will become an increasingly critical element of both strategy formulation and operational execution.

Most companies today are forced by competitive pressures to develop and adjust strategies almost continuously. It is much harder now to conceive a long-range plan and simply execute it to completion. Successful modern enterprises must often adjust their plans in real time to capitalize on the continuously changing environment, to take advantage of new opportunities as they arise and to avoid unforeseen pitfalls. Companies have always had to be nimble to succeed, but the imperative to become proactive gets stronger each day as business becomes more global and threats increase. Holding on to a competitive edge means staying one step ahead, and the more reliably one can predict the next step is often the difference between success and failure.

In the case of operational execution, the new challenge is not simply satisfying customer desires but accurately predicting what customers want before they know they want it! This means proactively ensuring customer satisfaction by making the buying experience predictably positive. At FedEx this means having the ability to update customers on the location of their shipments before they ask. We want to know as much as possible about each and every transaction so we can ensure delivery as promised and keep customers informed on a real-time basis.

The next step is to predict service disruptions before they occur, so we can re-route shipments or notify the customer as early as possible of any delay.

In the future, every company must be able to recognize what is coming early enough to take evasive action or steer toward an emerging opportunity. A continuous process of striving to extend one's field of view—as a pilot relies on radar for safe navigation—will be needed to see what's ahead. While no one can fully predict the future, information can be used to improve foresight on an ongoing basis. *The Power to Predict* challenges managers to think about the use of technology and information to augment historical analysis and business intelligence to produce better results.

Frederick W. Smith
Chairman & CEO
FedEx Corporation

PREFACE

IN *THE POWER OF NOW*™, I wrote about a world where information is available in real time; a world where information is delivered when it is needed to the people who need it, where decisions can be made at the point where they have the greatest impact, where operational agility is optimized, where customer service really means "service" and where the results show world-class performance.

Many people told me their business didn't operate like a trading floor. They didn't believe that real-time data was important in their business. But, sure enough, the term "real time" has become a standard for emphasizing the fact that you're receiving information as it happens. We have real-time traffic alerts, real-time weather and real-time news reports. The term is used ubiquitously to clarify active information. And now, real time applies to every industry in some shape or form.

Six years after *The Power of Now*, deploying real-time information delivery is not enough. Customers are telling me they need to detect, understand and manage business events in ways that lead to reliable, predictable results. And they have to do this in a world where complexity in both business and IT environments is constantly growing. *The Power to Predict*™ addresses how seemingly insignificant situations can now be correlated, interpreted and processed in ways we never thought possible.

I can tell you with great confidence that the Predictive Business principles discussed in this book are so visionary that certain customers we spoke with are unwilling to disclose how they are planning to apply them. Some are just beginning to think about the concepts while others, we suspect, are already quite advanced in their implementation. Regardless, there's a minimal amount of public documentation on the subject today—not because Predictive Business methodologies are not being used but because many executives believe their vision provides a competitive advantage and they are not ready to share it with the world.

In this book, I draw on my own company's experience in enabling the event-driven enterprise, as well as that of our customers and other industry drivers. And, I provide the answer to today's central question: "How can I harness all the things I know about my customers, my processes, my resources and my corporate assets to ensure my company's long-term prosperity?"

Vivek Ranadivé
Palo Alto, California

ACKNOWLEDGMENTS

I WOULD LIKE TO THANK the many individuals who have helped to bring this project to fruition. I want to thank Ram Menon for helping me to transform my initial thoughts and working with me to make this endeavor possible. I also appreciate the hard work of Dan Ziman in tying the threads together, along with my research team of Dennis Howlett and Lori Magaro. My editor Louise Kehoe, for her dedication and patience. I am also grateful to several colleagues who spent time contributing their perspective and thoughts on many aspects of the book: Murray Rode, Don Adams, Matt Quinn, Michael Magaro, Scott Fingerhut, Hans Jespersen, Peter Tebbenhoff, Puneet Arora, Ricardo Gomez-Ulmke, Mahau Ma and many others.

Finally, I want thank Jennifer Quichocho my assistant, for her patience, follow-through, and coordination.

THE POWER
TO PREDICT

WHY PREDICTIVE BUSINESS TODAY?

R EAL-TIME BUSINESS, based on the collection of current data, has become the standard operating procedure for leading-edge companies over the past decade, enabling them to respond rapidly to changing business conditions. Now we are seeing a transition to what I call Predictive Business™, or the ability to anticipate business problems and opportunities and to act preemptively. Real-time business was about doing things faster. Predictive Business is about doing things you could not do before.

As Malcolm Gladwell postulated in *The Tipping Point*, granular events can build to the point of critical mass, from which something new emerges.[1] I believe that we have now reached that point in the real-time business arena. Our abilities to capture, analyze and recognize patterns in dynamic data have reached critical mass and now provide the ability to anticipate future business events with a high degree of probability. When combined with the flexibility and agility to act before an event occurs, this creates a powerful new way of conducting business.

Predictive Business will transform the way companies of all types are managed. It will have a broad and profound impact on business practices akin to that of the introduction of corporate networks linking desktop computers and servers in the 1980s. Before we had computer networks, every desktop was an island and information traveled between workers in reusable "memo" envelopes. Today, it is difficult even to imagine the inefficiencies and slower pace of pre-network days. But networks did not only accelerate business and make it more efficient, they also changed people's jobs and responsibilities, removed pieces of the organizational structure in many areas, expanded the organizational structure in others, reduced decision cycle times, enabled companies to collaborate more closely with their suppliers and distributors and led to improved customer service.

Similarly, Predictive Business signals a radical new way of orchestrating business processes with the benefit of foresight. Companies might, for example, be able to predict and prevent the loss of a customer to a competing supplier, anticipate rising demand for a particular product and boost production or initiate proactive measures to mitigate risks they see arising in the future. Predictive Business will transform management's realm of possibilities for change and change management. It will enable companies to invest in new product development with greater certainty of success because they will know what their customers want. Most importantly, it will enable companies to take advantage of new opportunities and to avoid pitfalls that might have cost them millions of dollars.

NEW BALL GAME

Predictive Business is a whole new ball game. It is not just about collecting more data or using more sophisticated analytics. Rather, it is about combining technologies, business techniques, and orchestrated processes to better leverage your corporate assets. Sports provide us with a good way to understand the value of Predictive Business. Think about your favorite team. They obviously know how the game works—the rules, scoring system, layout, and boundaries of the playing surface and so on. To be competitive, the team needs to excel in at least one aspect of the game and be pretty good in all others. They also scout opponents, analyzing their previous games to learn their strengths, weaknesses, and tendencies in certain situations. Does the team play better at home, on grass, against their own division, making them the odds-on favorite over a division rival? They gather intelligence on competing teams in the same way you might use market research to prepare for a new sales initiative.

During the game, the team attacks, defends, and tries to find ways to outflank the opponent, run up the score, and defend against the big play. In this regard, the team is like a real-time business—out there absorbing everything that is happening on the field and acting upon the information gathered.

Then, a situational play is ready for execution. The coaches have analyzed the opponent's previous defenses and noticed a new scheme being deployed. Your team's offense immediately calls for a pass down the middle. The opponent is caught off guard and is ill prepared to defend. Your favored team went into the play with a high degree of confidence that their tactics would work, based on of the outcome in similar previous situations. That's predictive execution.

So now the question becomes do you want to run your business like a championship sports team, taking the field with confidence and then observing and proactively searching for the perfect time to call your new trick play? Or do you want to run it like you are at a casual softball game, swinging for the fences at every pitch, regardless of the score, situation, or pitcher because it's fun and you're not keeping score anyway?

Are you still running your business relying on stagnant historical data because you've come to expect that it's the best you can do? Or are you rounding second base, paying close attention to your third-base coach for real-time information? He's your predictor, watching the outfielder running down the line, estimating the timing of the throw and the infielders moving into position.

To advance the state of business, companies must explore how, with the right principles and technology, they can leverage predictive techniques to create competitive advantage. If you take real-time events and correlate them with historical patterns, you *can* anticipate events that hold the potential for tremendous profit.

The retailer, for instance, may identify the best customers in its stores or online ready to make purchases today. These customers generally spend more, and leave happier, when they are recognized as valuable and presented with special offers, personalized to reflect their purchasing patterns.

Businesses are beginning to adopt this mode of operation with startling results. The convenience store chain 7-Eleven, for example, is using Predictive Business techniques to revamp its stores. By collecting and analyzing sales data, the company is dynamically matching store orders to customers' demands. "We've gone from having no idea what we were selling to predicting what customers want even before they know it," says David Podeschi, 7-Eleven's senior vice president for merchandising.[2] Similarly, Wal-Mart mines its masses of real-time and historical data to predict consumer buying patterns. Who would have guessed that strawberry Pop Tarts and beer would fly off the shelves when a hurricane warning was issued? Wal-Mart identified this trend and now stocks up on these as well as more practical items in hurricane season.[3]

Similarly, in the manufacturing arena, Predictive Business creates the ability not only to manage supply and demand chains but also to anticipate events that may cause changes in operations, distribution, or logistics, making it possible to take preemptive action.

In *20/20 Foresight: Crafting Strategy in an Uncertain World*, Hugh Courtney writes, "The truth is that uncertainty is not an all-or-nothing phenomenon. Even in the most uncertain business environments, analysis can usually penetrate the uncertainty and withdraw strategically relevant information."[4] Kevin McGee, research fellow at industry analyst Gartner, goes further. He argues that contrary to what many believe, it is possible to trace *all* major corporate disasters to causal events and factors that appear in history. He goes on to say that if companies used knowledge about those events at the time they arose, then outcomes could be predicted with an astonishing degree of accuracy.[5]

Although there are many situations beyond your control, your attention needs to focus on the things in this world that are measurable and actionable. Furthermore, we have found that when better business principles and technology are correctly applied, events can be controlled to your benefit. This will resonate for all companies where a "better context, sooner" predictor provides significant competitive advantages. If you take real-time events and correlate them with historical patterns, you *can* anticipate future events with greater accuracy.

WHAT IS PREDICTIVE BUSINESS?

If we take a bird's-eye view, then we see that Predictive Business is the result of a trend that started two decades ago. In the 1980s and the early 1990s, companies started to recognize that they must be tightly connected to suppliers in order to seamlessly deliver products and services to their customers—supply chain management became part of the business lexicon. The supply chain concept was a "build it and they will come" way of thinking.

But this grand idea proved to be limited when some prominent companies "built it," yet the customers didn't come. They had misjudged and improperly forecasted demand for their products and were left with a great deal of inventory that had to be written off. One of the most dramatic illustrations of the failure of supply chain management came in 2001 when Cisco Systems found itself holding huge inventories of components and unfinished goods, forcing a $2.2 billion write-off.[6] Although Cisco has since recovered and grown, its inability to detect and correct this problem before it became immense raised serious questions about the application of real-time business principles to a large, complex business that outsources its manufacturing operations. If a model real-time business that boasted about its ability to balance its books in 24 hours was unable to avoid such a setback, what did this mean for other businesses?

The next step in the evolution of business was the demand chain, the "build it when they come" way of thinking. Today, this model works for your neighborhood deli, where your favorite sandwich can be assembled in a matter of minutes. In the computer industry, Dell is well known for its build-to-order approach. Similarly, in Europe, automobiles are typically custom-ordered from the manufacturer. Yet build-to-order also has its limitations, notably not providing customers with the instant gratification of driving a new car off the dealer's lot or using that new computer the day it is purchased. Some would say that this model forces the inventory burden onto suppliers rather than creating a business model geared to meeting customer demand.

In contrast, Predictive Business enables what I call the *eager network*: "build it because you know they are coming." Using this concept, businesses can avoid the pitfalls of both the supply and demand chains. You don't have to stockpile inventory or force your suppliers to do so. Nor do you put yourself in a situation where you don't have enough of the right product at the right time, potentially losing business or the opportunity to win new business.

But how do you drill into uncertainties and turn them into opportunities? Predictive Business, fueled by real-time data, provides the answers, as I will explain.

REAL-TIME BUSINESS DRIVERS

Since the advent of the business computer, companies have been running on historical data (what I call "data at rest") stored in large repositories or data warehouses. Every day, more data poured into the warehouse, adding to the accumulated knowledge. This growing store of data provided a record of the past but was inadequate for making decisions about current or future situations even when business intelligence analytics were applied.

Then, as technology progressed, it provided the means to accelerate the flow of data passing around the world and around a company, providing decision makers with current, real-time data.

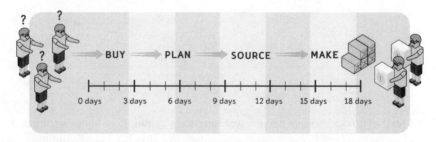

Demand Chain. The vendor focuses on build-to-order. Hence, customers don't actually receive the product when they request it.

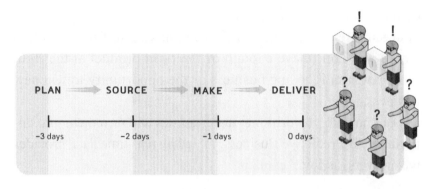

Supply Chain. Vendors try to optimize costs and improve margins by making large purchases at set intervals based on forecasted, aggregate buying behaviors. The results are that fewer customers get what they want, when they want it, or vendors are forced to carry more inventory than necessary.

Real-time business has changed the way executives approach strategic planning, changed the way managers allocate resources and changed the way line-level employees perform daily tasks. Implementing real-time techniques has had a profound effect on thousands of businesses by accelerating the pace of operations and enabling faster and more accurate decision-making.

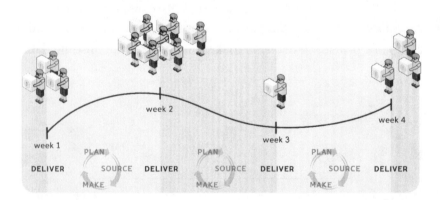

Eager Network. Vendors make fewer long-term assumptions about aggregate buying patterns and become more anticipatory to individual needs. Additionally, they are able to increase the number of plan, source and make cycles leading to customers obtaining products they want when they want them.

The value of real-time information can be seen in the quick resolution of production line problems, or the ability of a business to reroute in-transit inventory to where it is most needed or a consolidated production schedule for 30 manufacturing facilities in 20 countries across 15 time zones. It may mean redirecting the efforts of your sales force, adjusting your advertising to address new circumstances or shifting production to a new location. In all cases, it means responding rapidly to changing conditions based on up-to-the-minute business data.

Many people mistakenly think real-time information equals real-time business. This is not entirely true. Real-time business means having the ability to coordinate and control assets and activities at every level so you can sense and respond to change as it happens. This ensures your business is agile yet under control. I define real-time business as the ability to give customers what they want, when they want it, in the manner they want to receive it. Here are a few of my favorite examples demonstrating the value of real-time business:

It helped Pirelli gather order and sales data from thousands of suppliers and distributors worldwide, enabling the company to reduced excess inventory by 20 percent while increasing inventory throughput, leading to a 5 percent increase in revenues.

Adidas-Solomon implemented real-time business process management of their internal supply chain. They are now seeing reductions in processing costs with their suppliers while bringing new products to market faster.

Southwest Airlines upgraded its flight management system to provide pilots with guaranteed delivery of critical information, thus reducing flight delays and cancellations and improving the ability to meet the airline's stringent customer service requirements.

Real-time data helps you see what is happening right now. Often this is critical to business performance. For instance, understanding what a customer needs when the sales associate is across the counter may help develop an opportunity to up-sell. But you only know that an opportunity exists by processing and synthesizing the many signals that arise during the sales process. History helps draw the background canvas but it doesn't help fill in the foreground, where the action is taking place.

Historical data can be compared to an old photograph that captures a single moment in time, forever crystallizing it so people can examine it whenever they wish. But a single picture cannot put the recorded event in context. If you take multiple pictures in sequence and arrange them in an album, the relationship of one image to another over time becomes increasingly clear. This leaves the viewer with a substantially more complete idea of the event that actually occurred. But if we want to relate a series of historical events to the present, then what we need is a video camera, streaming real-time information to us in the present. This metaphor can apply to business-critical data, both historical and real-time, and it sets the scene for a transformational shift in how we regard data.

Twenty years ago, when I first got involved in building real-time information distribution systems for the trading floors of Wall Street, we were managing 600 events a second. Five years later, we were moving events over the network at a rate of 4,000 events per second. Now we're able to push a staggering 200,000 events a second to a broad set of recipients on an ever-increasing variety of devices. Today data flows from countless streams, providing a dynamic, three-dimensional depiction of what is happening *now*. Data is no longer inert, it's dynamic and fluid. It is "data in motion."

In both the past as well as today's business environments, managers are presented with the latest operations reports. But what is the real value of these documents? Only after a complete review can you finally make necessary business decisions. What about some of the poor results in the report—could you have implemented a business process the week before that would have prevented or at least mitigated the effect? If customers were not signing up for a new service you were actively promoting, you'd want to know as soon as possible. That way you could adjust your strategy, perhaps plug in a replacement offer and resume your monitoring immediately.

You now have that luxury. Using a correlated and integrated flow of information from sensors, routers and all other computer-based sources, you can trigger an immediate search for service issues across an entire region and assess the situation. You can then review the events that your customers experienced and the events that occurred when your customers called your service centers. You now have a real-time picture of the situation, in context. You are able to make truly informed decisions to resolve the current problem. If the issue you identify suggests a process change, you can now plan to ensure the problem is not replicated in the future. The result might well be millions of dollars *not* lost while you move on to proactively build the next, differentiated service offering.

TRANSITION TO PREDICTIVE BUSINESS

Companies will increasingly transition toward Predictive Business as they begin to look at business events in greater and greater detail and in tighter and tighter time frames. Using historical knowledge, you will create a set of standard patterns in which behaviors—of events, customers and transactions—will be identified. The next time you see this sequence of behaviors aligning in the same or similar fashion, you will know the likelihood that it will result in the same kind of outcome.

To achieve the highest level of success, the implementation of Predictive Business methods must be hard-baked into the company's infrastructure. Not only your IT infrastructure but also your business model, your operating plan and your corporate culture need to be aligned with Predictive Business. For senior managers, this means embracing Predictive Business techniques and demonstrating their commitment to this new approach, even if it also means relinquishing the role of the business sage whose "gut" feelings lead to good decisions.

I realize that not so long ago, when the world was running at a slower pace, really smart business people could put discrete business events together, say "Ah ha!" and then make the necessary business decisions. However, the accelerating pace and complexity of business make it extraordinarily difficult to have these "Ah ha!" moments. Increasingly, we rely upon technology to give us the information we need to make decisions. Today, I would estimate that about 30 percent of commercial business software incorporates presumptive scripting, invoking an automatic reaction when specific events occur. But over time, we will see a greater percentage of situations where the future is forecast by pattern recognition models. These models will take action instantly to keep us ahead of the event curve.

It will mean that some decision-making will fall out of human hands. But people will design alternative pattern recognition scenarios within a given business model. Those models and their projected outcomes will be tested. Then decision makers will have an array of outcomes from which to select the most likely scenario in a given set of circumstances.

NO PAIN, NO GAIN

A friend of mine remarked that leaders must need a great deal of vision to incorporate Predictive Business into operations. I replied that it isn't so much about vision as it is about relieving the pain of missed opportunities, unforeseen problems and unanticipated expenses. Pain is a big motivator when it comes to revolutionizing the way we do business. One example arose when a prospective telco client told me, "We need to reduce our customer churn. How can this be fixed?" Another was when a very large consumer goods company approached me to ask, "How can we ensure that our products are on supermarket shelves whenever consumers want to buy them?"

Despite millions of dollars spent on technology, these companies' pain points were not being adequately addressed. The volumes of data they were collecting kept growing, but they did not have the technology to integrate the immediate capture of a complex event and a corresponding counter-tactic. The computing model was database-centric, which meant people needed to know everything up front, organize all that information and somehow create a monstrous database to accommodate it. On top of this, businesses were required to use hard-wired, point-to-point connections between business applications. *Then*, if anything changed, which it inevitably did with increasing frequency, everything had to be redesigned, recoded, retested and redeployed. Fortunately, technology has progressed since then.

We are now in the age of process-centric computing, an age in which integrated systems share data. The resulting correlations between data and processes provide a more complete and contextual picture of situations. Businesses can adapt their way of doing things without interrupting operations. The right information flows to and through the enterprise to get wherever it needs to be, when-

Volume. As the Internet boomed, so did the volume of information. Dubbed by media as "information overload."

Volume + Variety. More recently, the types of information sent to users have grown substantially making it more difficult to quickly discern opportunities and threats.

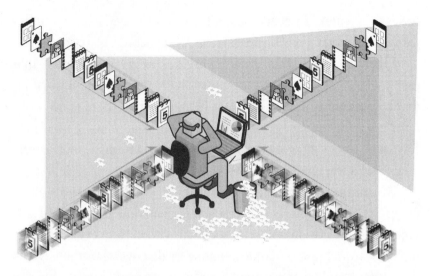

Volume + Variety + Velocity. Now, as organizations build out the infrastructure to support information access, many are unprepared for the exponential increase in the speed at which operations execute.

ever it needs to be there. In addition, the latest wave of information technology has allowed businesses to remove communication and performance barriers.

Predictive Business is the next leap forward. It will enable companies to simulate, model and manage business processes. It will also enable us to *reverse-engineer* events, starting with the pain (or the desired gain) and working backwards to the discrete events that caused the pain point in the first place. Businesses will be able to go back and look at the subatomic particles of a transaction and to see what went right or wrong. It then becomes possible to see how alternative business processes might be deployed to obviate the problem or take advantage of the opportunity. Moving forward, the process can be modeled and monitored for an event, the absence of an event or a pre-set event threshold. You can then take standard actions with existing assets and standard operations, based on a series or a pattern of events that allows you to say, "I've seen it before" and modify your business processes accordingly.

Likewise, companies are creating business "dashboards" that display key performance indicators (KPIs) to provide a warning that something is amiss or assure managers that there is no problem. These dashboards can alert the appropriate managers if performance trends suggest that contractual obligations—such as service level agreements (SLAs)—may be missed.

Businesses may also apply metrics to create warning signals using Six-Sigma quality processes to gain an understanding of service thresholds or outcomes associated with certain events. Working back from these outcomes, managers discover the small events that either enable them to meet their business standards or give rise to service failures.

Adopting new business techniques is challenging. It involves constantly adjusting to changing conditions. Think of this in terms of driving over a mountain pass with hairpin bends during a rainstorm. You must always be alert and you need to steer carefully, adjusting your acceleration and braking to ensure that you do not miss the next curve in the road.

So how are you going to take advantage of Predictive Business? How will you convert information into knowledge across your enterprise? And from there, how will you turn knowledge into action?

If you can make the necessary adjustments to your business's course, you can keep the Predictive Business-based organization on the road to success. The benefits of Predictive Business are significant. The requirements and responsibilities are demanding. You and everyone in your company will have the information you need to make smart decisions and your business will be technically agile enough to adapt and avoid a crash. As a leader, you need to ensure that your corporate culture and every member of your team are onboard with the need for constant change, so they are willing to embrace continuous improvements.

A NEW KIND OF LEADER

It's going to take a different kind of leader to champion Predictive Business. It will demand someone who is comfortable saying that Predictive Business will require us to view our businesses from new angles. Additionally, there are important philosophies this new leader should embrace:

- If you really want to be competitive in the market, real time is no longer good enough. You've got to be thinking ahead and acting on what *might* be happening.

- If you can't place individual events into the proper context, reacting to them will only provide marginal value.

- There are virtually endless possibilities on how you could use Predictive Business in your industry.

- You need to understand the dependencies between events— what each event means and what its impact is on the business.

- It's not always about the big "Ah ha!" moment. It's really about constantly measuring, correlating, predicting and adjusting.

- Strive for simplicity. If the answer is as complex as the pain you're trying to relieve, it will never be actionable.

The Power to Predict is neither fanciful nor mystical. It is becoming a reality more quickly than many people think. I get a sense of déjà vu when discussing these concepts, because real time was met with skepticism and thought to be just as strange back then as Predictive Business may be today. But history proved that my assumptions were correct. The answers to questions such as "Why is real time important?" and "Who really needs to embrace real time?" came quickly and were just as swiftly validated.

In 1989, Gary Hamel and C. K. Prahalad wrote, "Strategic intent is like a marathon run in 400-meter sprints. No one knows what the terrain will look like at mile 26, so the role of the top management is to focus the organization's attention on the ground to be covered in the next 400 meters."[7]

The next 400-meter leg of the race is in front of us. How are you going to run it? Will you embrace Predictive Business and leverage its power to propel you to the winner's circle? How can you guarantee you will finish ahead of the crowd? In the following chapters, I will provide answers.

THE SUCCESS OF THE REAL-TIME BUSINESS

THE POWER OF NOW

The foundations of Predictive Business lie in the real-time technologies, processes and practices that I described in *The Power of Now*, back in 1999. At that time, it was difficult for many people to believe in a world of intelligently connected systems that all understood one another. We were at the height of the dot-com bubble, and there was much talk of global "B2B" marketplaces being built on the Web. Siebel Systems was growing rapidly as large corporations adopted customer relationship management software to gather customer data and create incentive and loyalty programs. Sun Microsystems had just launched its Jini technology that promised to enable any device to link to the network. And TIBCO Software Inc. was pioneering the use of real-time data to enable "e-business," as we then called it.

Businesses were rushing to adapt to the Internet, yet there was still a lot of skepticism about the value of real-time information. The general feeling was that real time was only for super high-powered traders on Wall Street and very few people could see how it might apply to a broader spectrum of businesses. It was much like the early days of the personal computer when many people said, "Well, why would I ever need a home computer?" It was impossible then for most people to imagine children using PCs to do their homework or for vacationers to book their travel online and store their digital photos on a PC when they got home.

Similarly, the real-time bandwagon has rolled a long way in the past five or six years. Many industries and businesses have implemented real-time technologies and derived tremendous dollar value from doing so. What is more, the principles of real-time operations are now firmly established as core components of business success. Today you would be hard pressed to find a business that doesn't comprehend that it is essential to be able to serve customers on a timely basis, to manage supply chains on a timely basis and to be able to respond to threats and opportunities on a timely basis.

Whether you are running an airline or a financial services institution, or you are a retailer or a computer manufacturer, you need to be able to run your business in an integrated real-time fashion. However, one of the inevitable consequences of the broad adoption of real-time technologies is that the term *real time* has come to mean many different things to different people, in part because the IT industry is faddish in its adoption of new terminology and overuse inevitably leads to distortions.

I will begin a review of real time by giving you a clear definition: Real time means making *necessary* information available to the *people* or *systems* that need it, *when* they need it and in a way in which they can act *effectively* upon that information. Ultimately, it is about having the ability to make faster and better decisions than competitors. By having ready access to information and superior mechanisms to process it, the real-time enterprise fundamentally improves operational efficiency, outsmarts competitors and con-

DBS Bank's Growing Services

DBS Bank is one of the largest financial services groups in Asia. Beyond its home market in Singapore, the state-owned bank serves corporate, institutional and retail customers through its operations in Hong Kong, Thailand, the Philippines, Indonesia, and China. DBS has dominant positions in consumer banking, treasury and markets, securities brokerage, equity, and debt fund raising.

As DBS started to grow its franchise, it saw the need to build a technology platform that promoted business agility. Systems at DBS were connected by point-to-point interfaces that had to be maintained and modified with time-consuming and error-prone coding. And because very few of these interfaces were reusable, the company had to spend significant resources duplicating logic and infrastructure for key services such as phone and Internet banking in each channel and market. In addition, DBS had to build duplicate and costly components such as identity and security modules for each new application.

Instead of attempting to fix integration issues piecemeal, DBS opted to rebuild its technology foundation using a service-oriented architecture (SOA) so that it would provide the agility required to capture market opportunities while simultaneously reducing IT costs and improving consistency.

Reuse of Services Facilitates Regional Growth

DBS standardized its back-office services and implemented new front-end applications such as the corporate Internet banking application. However, at the top of the team's agenda is a plan to build services that encapsulate the bank's major applications. These reusable services will enable DBS to quickly and cost-effectively reproduce distinct versions of its customer-facing applications for use in different countries from a shared library of back-office services.

"By providing a predictable, standard way to perform integration and create services, we were able to reduce the time and resources needed to integrate new systems into our standard platform," says Richard Anderson, managing director of the information technology group, DBS Bank. "We expect that this will make it easier for DBS to deliver superior and consistent customer services in every new market we enter."

Strategic Initiatives

The ability to integrate applications rapidly has helped improve the time-to-market for DBS products and given the company the agility it needs to react to changing market conditions.

"To be a leading market player, we must act quickly to take advantage of market trends and to seize new opportunities," Anderson says. "Now if an organization wants to operate a service in partnership with us—such as payment processing—we can integrate the necessary systems quickly and provide that service to the customer at a reasonable cost."

Lower Costs

DBS has also been able to lower costs in several areas. The bank has realized an unanticipated 50 percent cost savings in file transfer management. The maintenance and support costs for integration components were also cut in half. By using an enterprise integration platform rather than point-to-point integration, costs on another software development project were cut by 20 percent.

"We are now in a better position to suggest innovative cost-saving business solutions," says Anderson. DBS is now executing a three-year road map to consolidate regional banking applications to improve operational quality and reduce costs.

tinually senses and drives new revenue streams. But let us consider real time as it applies to some specific situations and industries.

When an aircraft's sensors detect a fault in a real-time environment, a message needs to get to the right people as quickly as possible so that corrective action can be taken. In practical terms, it means assembling the right maintenance crew and parts so that when the plane lands, the crew is able to take care of the problem immediately. There may be a practical limit on the amount of time between the sensor relaying its message to ground control and the start of the repair process, but real-time systems provide maintenance with enough information and the maximum time window to efficiently assemble all the necessary parts.

On the other hand, when a passenger reaches the front of a Delta Airlines check-in line, real time means the agent is pulling up the customer's travel history, seating preferences, dietary requirements and so on within two or three seconds. Delta check-in staff know not only the extent to which each customer travels, they know how profitable each is. This is because customer information is tied into Delta's financial systems. Armed with this information, check-in staff can immediately identify their best customers and act appropriately to ensure that the customer enjoys a differentiated experience.

Switching to the financial markets, real-time information is vital in stock trading. To cite an extreme example, NASDAQ processes about 60,000 messages a second. Each of these messages must be audited to ensure that all information on every trade is delivered within an SEC-mandated time frame. But when NASDAQ stock traders are operating, they need information almost instantly.

In each case, real-time technology is used to accomplish a business goal. While the time interval varies, it is essential that information be delivered *fast enough*. So for every organization, real time means delivering information at the *right* time.

Wall between IT and Business. The demands of business units create significant pressure on the IT organization. Often, what may appear to be simple
requests for timely information are in fact more complex due to the back-end
systems and legacy applications. Analysts serve as intermediaries between
business requests and IT delivery.

CUSTOMER CRITICAL

Real-time performance is critical for companies to meet their
goals of acquiring, retaining and growing loyal customers. This is
because we live in a world of instant gratification, fueled by the

ubiquitous availability of information about products and services. In the world of Internet consumerism, your average user is more knowledgeable about products and services than ever before and will tolerate nothing less than exemplary execution. So customers' demands are driving the push to real time. From a business perspective, real time is no longer optional. Your business survival means assimilating and executing against a real-time mindset. But be careful.

Gathering more information from more sources does not, in itself, guarantee the success of a real-time operation. In many ways, the tsunami of information that real-time environments can deliver creates new challenges. Now you must disseminate, route, and filter vastly greater volumes of information more rapidly than ever before.

Indeed, implementing real-time techniques successfully is by no means trivial. Different business processes and the systems that support them often operate in isolation, unaware of the knowledge that resides elsewhere in the enterprise network. Yet the true benefits of real time emerge only when systems are coordinated. There may, for example, be orders, returns, inventory, in-process inventory and in-transit inventory. One plane arrives today with product, another product is being unloaded, more arrive in a week and some already reside in the distribution channel. Sorting through this information and figuring out which customers should be served first based on customer priority, shipping efficiency, required date, etc., require that all systems be synchronized.

Given the complexity (and possible costs), why go to the trouble? Will it be worth it? How long before my business sees a payback and what's so wrong with answering the customer tomorrow or the next day? As I've already said, customers won't tolerate what they perceive as unnecessary delay in providing an appropriate re-

Latent, Undetected Customer Service Needs are Simply Not Tolerated.
Organizations often wrestle to understand the importance and value of moving to a real-time and event-driven infrastructure. Yet, when we think of our everyday lives, notions of set intervals and batch processing are significantly out of place. Events will dictate the course of action, not the interval at which services are offered.

sponse. I'd go one step further. Success in the business world is not only about having the greatest product superbly marketed alongside the most trusted brand. It's also about giving the customer the best, differentiated service you possibly can, learning from customer interactions and then acting upon those interactions.

CHARACTERISTICS OF REAL-TIME COMPANIES

During the many years I've spent assisting companies in implementing real-time systems, I have observed that without exception, they all display certain common characteristics:

Customer-driven—They define themselves as being, above all else, customer-centric. Concern for the customer permeates all their technology and policy decisions. They embrace the Internet, the World Wide Web and the more traditional channels such as mail and fax to ensure customers can conduct business with them in the most convenient, effective and profitable manner.

Embrace cultural change—They embrace the cultural change required to move from a collection of information silos to a cross-functional structure in which rich information flows transparently between operational managers. They recognize that change of this degree can inflame turf battles and scare those used to hoarding information. Therefore, they find ways to resolve these issues. While committed to placing the best management information tools in the hands of their employees, they share information on a "need to know" basis and enforce data security rules.

Management by exception—These companies implement policies, procedures, and rules that support management by exception. Because so many processes are automated, it becomes necessary to emphasize and ensure there is a support structure in place to respond effectively to exceptions. Although the exceptions represent a small

Pirelli Reduces Supply Chain Risk

"We now have visibility throughout the supply chain. We've increased productivity, reduced costs and improved our time-to-market with new products."

—Dario Scagliotti, CIO, Pirelli

Trucks, buses, sports cars, family sedans, motorcycles, and tractors all roll on Pirelli tires, which are manufactured in 10 countries and sold in 120. All major automobile manufacturers mount Pirellis as original equipment. However, most of the tire division's $4.2 billion in 2004 revenue came from a worldwide network of 6,000 distributors and dealers.

Tire manufacturing is a challenging business. Tires are commodity products with traditionally low profit margins and competitors crowd the market. Yet Pirelli, one of the leading tire companies in the world, is moving closer to the lead due in part to an integrated infrastructure spanning the enterprise and dealer network, helping the company win distributor loyalty and build market share.

Pirelli's system includes supply chain management, production planning and finance applications shared with Pirelli's thousands of distributors worldwide. To streamline supply chain management and cut operating costs, Pirelli needed to link these disparate applications.

Reduced Risk Allows Pirelli to Speed Ahead

Custom integrations are risky projects that can be time-consuming to develop, test and stabilize. The Pirelli integration team also needed to establish compatibility among several different distributor systems. Many small local dealers transacted business by fax and paper; large national and regional distributors used sophisticated combinations of enterprise resource planning (ERP) and custom applications. By adopting a common infrastructure for linking all of these systems, Pirelli eliminated the need for custom interfaces and streamlined the integration process.

Pirelli's internal business applications—including multiple instances of SAP and homegrown applications—were integrated providing a common conduit for sharing information. Pirelli now quickly integrates distributors with an online order entry and tracking system. On average, Pirelli can connect large distributors to the Pirelli System in two weeks and can bring small dealers online in as little as one hour by giving them access to a personalized Web-based portal for self service. In less than a year, Pirelli connected 2,500 distributors—an accomplishment that has accelerated the payback on its integration investment.

Loyalty among Distributors Increases Sales

The convenience of Pirelli's online order system results in distributors transacting more business with the tire manufacturer, giving it a competitive edge. The system provides easy access to the latest pricing information, fast and simple online order entry and immediate confirmation. In addition, distributors now know exactly when shipments will arrive and can track orders online. With real-time information about order status, distributors can serve their own customers better.

"We now have a more complete, richer way of working together with our distribution partners," says Dario Scagliotti, CIO of Pirelli. As a result, every time Pirelli has integrated a distributor into the system, the company's sales have increased.

Managed Inventory Boosts Revenues and Reduces Costs

Pirelli also implemented a supply chain management system. This was a top priority because the firm finances inventory at distributor locations, so excess inventory increases its costs. However if inventory is too low, Pirelli risks losing sales to its competitors.

Pirelli can now match inventory to sales by automating order entry and processing. The system alerts distributors when their inventory of high-volume products is low and automatically generates replenishment orders. This cuts the time required to deliver replacement tires to a distributor, while maintaining distributor stocking levels and avoiding excessive inventory.

Since implementing its integrated supply chain management system, Pirelli has reduced distributor inventories by 20 percent and cut its own costs. Sales are rarely lost because a tire is out of stock or back ordered. After implementing the new distributor capabilities, sales have already climbed 5 percent, increasing Pirelli's market share.

Pirelli Synchronizes Production to Demand

Pirelli's integrated supply chain management system has improved forecasting and production planning, giving the company the agility to respond to market dynamics. Pirelli once required 70 days to poll its thousands of distributors for sales forecasts, collect the information that trickled in on paper, aggregate the information and manually generate production plans. In the meantime, demand could change and render production plans obsolete. Now, with up-to-the-minute information on orders and inventory levels, the entire process is completed in just 30 minutes. Pirelli no longer depends on quarterly forecasts. Using real-time sales data, the supply chain can adjust production rapidly to match sales.

Real-Time Information Keeps Business on Track

The process of collecting, sorting, analyzing, and reporting key performance indicators for Pirelli previously consumed 90 days. Now the process takes just 30 minutes. Company executives can see up-to-the-minute performance indicators at a company, business unit or product level. With real-time information available throughout the enterprise, Scagliotti says decision makers can now navigate Pirelli more skillfully—and lead the company to the finish line faster.

"We can manage our business only as far as we can see it," Scagliotti says. "We now have visibility throughout the supply chain. We've increased productivity, reduced costs and improved our time-to-market with new products."

fraction of the total volume of business, managers must remain accountable because these are companies that do not tolerate lapses in customer support or sloppy operations.

Innovation—These are not meek companies. They do not shy away from change. They react swiftly and easily to changing conditions to retain and grow market share. In fact, they see each change as an opportunity to utilize their superior response capabilities to gain market share from their competitors. They also realize that nothing lasts forever so they are constantly searching for new ideas.

Merit-based alliances—These companies do not form alliances or interlocking relationships in the conventional sense. For them, the concept of static business relationships based on outmoded contracts is meaningless. Instead, relationships with suppliers and partners change quickly and unapologetically. Change doesn't happen on a whim but it is accepted as an inevitable part of valued long-term relationships.

Meritocratic and entrepreneurial—These companies are not consensus-oriented. Instead, they are meritocratic and fiercely entrepreneurial, preferring star employees to team players. Most importantly, they freely provide all the tools their people need to *become* stars.

Leaders provide opportunity—Leaders don't empower workers. Instead, they organize the company so that workers can empower themselves. They encourage workers to risk failure rather than accept mediocrity and the status quo. In turn, their staff is not afraid to make mistakes.

Short planning cycles—Event-driven companies' planning horizons are usually one year or less. They initially use a short

cycle time to focus resources on the invention, production
and delivery of a product or service. Once proven, the
cycle expands outward to capture long-term value.

Finally, all of these businesses employ what I call an "event-driven
architecture."

BUILDING THE FRAMEWORK

The event-driven architecture (EDA) is the vital IT framework of
real-time business. In an EDA, information is available from, and
can be transmitted to, all nodes on the network. New information
derived from analytical programs can also be fed back to the network for further consumption.

On a micro basis, each business unit absorbs its relevant information and feeds it back to the network to be utilized by other
interested parties. On a macro basis, the EDA turns information
into corporate knowledge and, with the appropriate processes in
place, makes that knowledge actionable. Isolated islands of information don't exist in an EDA. The entire organization makes decisions and acts upon up-to-date and complete information.

It is important to recognize the difference between an EDA and
the traditional "request/reply" approach in which users must determine where information is stored and then request a copy. Finding
the right information is a hit-and-miss task and there is no guarantee that it will be the most up-to-date version or exactly what the
user wants. We have all experienced, for example, the flotsam
served up by Internet search engines that were designed to help to
automate the request/reply model.

In contrast, an EDA automatically serves up fresh and relevant
information to each user on a corporate network without anybody
requesting, for example, a report or an update. On the Internet, ser-

vices such as Google's news alert (which e-mails news on a specific topic) are closer to what I mean by an EDA. However, Google alerts still require users to specify which topics they want to hear about, while a corporate EDA will automatically select relevant topics based on the job functions of an individual.

A business with EDA makes decisions with the latest information, enabling it to respond much faster to any change. The business becomes a learning company, because each activity that occurs is analyzed by the entire network. It can then spot trends and act upon them in real time. Moreover, the EDA does not stop at the boundaries of the internal business network. It may consume and process information from customers and other third parties.

The EDA is fundamental to real-time operation and provides the underpinnings of Predictive Business.

THE BIRTH OF REAL TIME

The real-time epiphany came for me in the mid-1980s when I first walked onto the trading floor of a major New York brokerage house. Deregulation had transformed this industry. Until the early 1980s, trading commissions were set by the government, giving traders a comfortable margin. Effectively, it was a protected market where traders could virtually guarantee a comfortable return. When government regulation ended, discount brokerages slashed commissions, members of the public awoke to the need to invest their own money (rather than rely on pensions) and it was off to the races. By the mid-1980s, the volume of shares traded daily on the New York Stock Exchange was running at around 100 million trades per day. This was 20 times the volumes seen in the 1960s.

But technology had not kept up and was swamped by the sheer volume. Each trader had a dozen or more screens broadcasting incompatible data. From those screens, a twisted mess of cables snaked to the floor. If a single cable was accidentally unplugged, several neighboring screens went dead. When a trader moved desks, the IT staff had to move the entire setup. The trading process itself was slow. On average, it took over 20 separate keyboard entries to record the details of a single securities purchase. As I looked at this jumble of out-of-control, incompatible equipment, I realized that order could be brought to this chaotic environment by adopting a distributed computing solution I had been developing.

In the computer hardware world, standard components are plugged in to the "chassis" of circuit boards known as the "bus." I posed the question, "Why not build a software bus—one that makes it possible to plug together software modules of any kind?" At the time, the IT department of the brokerage was highly skeptical. This had never been tried before.

My fledgling company built this software solution, which I named The Information Bus™ (TIB™). Briefly stated, an information (or service) bus is to software what the bus is to hardware. It is a central, universal conduit to which components and applications can be connected. Regardless of their language or technology, these components and applications communicate and interoperate with each other.

We realized early on that there was a need to allow these intercommunications to occur dynamically and transparently. We addressed this by equipping the information bus with a way to distribute messages based on their content. This meant that we did not need to know or track all of the parties that might be interested in a change to a specific stock price. Rather we let parties subscribe to the information that was of interest to them so they could receive information as often as it changed. Say, for example, a trader is interested in General Electric's share price. When the price changes, the information bus publishes it once and all parties subscribing to this information automatically receive the new share price. However, a trader is typically interested in much more than simple price movements, so we had to work out a way of managing and presenting *all* the information pertinent to individual stocks. This might include historical data such as General Electric's trading volumes over a specified period or breaking news about the company. The information might be displayed as charts, graphs, text or running numbers. When a trader responds to that data, his or her actions are reported instantly. But there was still something missing.

I was convinced that we could eliminate the mess of hardware by presenting all the information on a single screen. My first opportunity to realize this dream came in 1987, when we proposed a distributed system to Fidelity Investments—one in which each trader would have his or her own personal workstation rather than a dumb terminal connected to the mainframe.

To test this, we researched every conceivable action and reaction that would be triggered by changes in the price of a stock. Then we blended and collated live data streaming in from up to 25 different news-reporting sources. Next we presented coherent real-time reports, in both text and charts, and tracked the outward rippling impact of each potential trading action. For the first time, the trader had all the information required to create maximum value, delivered instantaneously to a single screen. That information bypassed the mainframe and sped directly to a desktop workstation. It blew Fidelity away.

In the early '80s and mid-'90s we worked with hundreds of leading corporations, including a significant portion of the financial services industry. Reuters embedded software into its information services products, where it became the backbone for Reuters's news-reporting services.

The information bus established Wall Street as an efficient, real-time industry. Real time was sorely needed there because deregulation had transformed a high profit, slow moving industry to a low margin, furiously paced one. Deregulation had given birth to the commoditization of share trading. In my view, it is a combination of commoditization and the innovative use of technology by competitors that leads to what I call the "rust belt." This is a phenomenon where creeping commoditization and technology use by competitors erodes a company's ability to sustain its established business model, just as rust erodes metal. In some cases, entire business models are rendered obsolete. One need only consider the impact of Amazon on the book publishing market to realize that the rust belt is real and dangerous. Those companies that do not respond to the threat perish because new, nimble entrants to their market disrupt the status quo.

PROLIFERATING THE INFORMATION BUS

As we developed this transformational method of delivering information, I realized that the power of this technology was more than a mere unraveling of twisted data. It was a logical compounding of information that grew richer at each turn. I saw that we could augment the simple reporting fluctuations in stock prices by feeding those price-change reports into application programs to create wide-ranging analyses and then automated trading decisions. These higher functions in turn created new data, which we instantaneously fed back into the network for other traders to use. The result was an upward spiraling, endless, closed feedback loop of incrementally enriched, refined, and integrated information. This signaled the birth of the event-driven, competitively differentiated company.

From here, it was a small step to realizing that an information bus was of value to not only the financial services industry but to any kind of business. At its heart, the key to real-time operations was closed loop, continuous information feedback. You can instantaneously look at what is being sold, determine where it is being sold and analyze the sales mix. The time spent reviewing this information is cut drastically, and accuracy is greatly improved because information is managed and orchestrated based on events that impact change. With this technology, fundamental business processes such as forecasting, pricing, manufacturing and store stocking can be constantly monitored and adjusted to changing circumstances.

THE POWER TO PREDICT

WHAT EXACTLY DO I MEAN by *The Power to Predict?* Primarily, I believe that Predictive Business does two things. First, it helps you seize opportunities as they are unfolding. Perhaps you've said to yourself, "I know what's about to happen." With Predictive Business, you can be much more definitive. Second, it allows you to anticipate adverse conditions so that seemingly small and unrelated events do not become the precursors to disaster. It's extremely rare that major events suddenly happen with no warning signs, small events or out-of-tolerance situations. Correlating those items will allow you to take preemptive action.

There are several prerequisites to operating as a Predictive Business:

I am making a fundamental assumption that exemplary execution against best-practice customer satisfaction is the company's mantra.

None of us has a crystal ball to foresee the future. But seizing opportunities and avoiding missteps should be routine.

Events can be captured, analyzed, and acted upon. You must, of course, be motivated and ready to take up the challenge.

Events don't happen in isolation. They are the culmination of event patterns, which can be recognized and understood through careful analysis of both historical and real-time data.

Thoroughly understanding the unique business processes that give the company its edge is critical, as is the ability to change those processes at will.

The best performing companies are self-aware, learning organizations where change is an accepted part of daily life.

A Predictive Business does not sit on its laurels. Competitive advantage is maintained through continuing advances, each of which provides a temporary edge.

Before diving into more detail, I should say something about what Predictive Business isn't. It is emphatically *not* about ditching past investments, nor is it about ripping out the old and replacing with something new. It will take an investment in human resources and technology. But the rewards and the upside potential are huge. When I talk to company leaders about Predictive Business, I often see the "light bulb effect." They recognize the potential of this approach and see it as a natural progression of real-time business practices.

An efficient and flexible IT infrastructure capable of capturing events and data in real time is also a prerequisite for Predictive Business. However, technology doesn't provide silver bullets. There has to be top-level motivation, a will to succeed and a willingness to try new things. Some will work and some won't. When people ask broad questions like, "How can we influence customers' behavior so they stay loyal to our brand?" or, "What's missing in the marketplace that we could maybe do?" then the company is at the start of that transformational process. I once heard a CEO who exhorted his management team in the following terms: "I want you to come up with ten ideas a week. I don't care that nine-and-a-half of them are crazy. We'll make fortunes for the company out of the half an idea that works." Those are the words of someone who is fostering innovation, imagination, and risk-taking.

PREDICTING THE NOW

Perfect knowledge doesn't exist. We may think it exists; we may wish for it, but the reality is different. If we are to be effective as business managers, then we have to be rooted in what is achievable now.

We cannot, for instance, be 100 percent sure what will happen at any one time. At the most minute level, I cannot know with any certainty that human frailty or natural disaster will not interrupt my business. I may get ill. One of my key employees may be in a car accident. My office building may be without power or traffic may prevent me from attending a critical customer meeting. These are the kinds of unpredictable events that none of us can foresee. In some cases, we may be able to predict an event, but not its magnitude or the effect it will have. Hurricane Katrina and the tsunami in Southeast Asia are recent examples.

We may have contingency plans in place—a deputy who can take my place if I am unwell, a deep bench of executives who can stand in for one another, backup plans for emergency office accommodation and perhaps even a "hot site" that duplicates my critical data center functions. If I cannot attend a meeting in person, I might have a video conferencing facility at the ready.

Most of us make some contingency plans as we strive to control the future but it is impossible to plan for every eventuality. In business transactions, the story is much more complex because generally there are numerous actual and potential variables. Since we are inevitably engaged in complex relationships with other people, it is pointless to seek 100 percent predictability. We intuitively know that people are by their very nature unpredictable. It is what defines us as humans and provides the backdrop for diversity.

What we should and *can* do, however, is embrace uncertainty to clarify those events over which we can exercise a degree of control. We should analyze past and real-time events to spot patterns, so we can take corrective actions for future events in ways that lead to desirable outcomes. We are, in essence, reducing the level of uncertainty to manageable proportions and ensuring that we will "get it right" more often than in the past.

It is time to cast aside skepticism about the opportunity to predict outcomes and avoid negative business consequences. Leading thinkers in this field such as David Luckham, Stanford professor and author of *The Power of Events*, and Ken McGee of Gartner Inc., author of *Heads Up*, have provided significant evidence that Predictive Business is ready for prime time. My own conversations with executives have further proven that they can detect and take action in ways they never thought possible even two or three years ago. Let's explore the science of prediction a bit further.

THE SCIENCE OF PREDICTION

During the 1960s, meteorologist Edward Lorenz stumbled across patterns of events that were eventually embodied in chaos theory. He found what has since become known as the "butterfly effect." Mathematician Ian Stewart described the phenomenon as follows: "The flapping of a single butterfly's wing today produces a tiny change in the state of the atmosphere. Over time, what the atmosphere actually does diverges from what it would have done. In a month's time, a tornado that would have devastated the Indonesian coast doesn't happen. Or maybe one that wasn't going to happen, does."[1] This phenomenon, common to chaos theory, is also known as sensitive dependence on initial conditions. Just a small change in the initial conditions (events) can drastically change the long-term behavior of a system.

Science has since demonstrated that despite the apparently chaotic state of the world, there is order in chaos; randomness has an underlying geometrical form. Chaos imposes fundamental limits on prediction, but it also suggests causal relationships where none was previously suspected. In chaotic systems, since there is no clear relation between cause and effect, such phenomena are said to have random elements.

In the real world, stock price movements appear to be random— and in the short term, they are. Some describe the trading floor as little more than a glorified casino, where chance plays a significant role in determining price movements. But observation has revealed long-term, deterministic behavior. This is because stock prices are influenced by real events and not merely sentiment interacting with the economics of supply and demand. Chaos theory might imply that the value of real time in the trading floor environment is limited, but experience shows that isn't true. When traders have access to real-time information, they are equipped to update their trading models in a fraction of the time it would otherwise take and so make decisions within acceptable, measurable levels of risk.

EVENT PROBABILITY

Statistical analysis proves that events can be predicted within given levels of probability. While we may not be able to predict everything that impacts business, we can measure, manage, control, and respond to at least some of the business-critical events that occur during the customer life cycle. There is nothing new about this. Statistical analysis gives us, for example, the "mean time before failure" of mechanical equipment. Actuaries, similarly, use statistical analysis to set life insurance rates.

In everyday life, we can predict with a fair degree of certainty that the time taken to make a given journey to the office will be, say, 45 minutes. But we cannot be 100 percent certain because there might be a traffic accident at a busy intersection that doubles the journey time. What we can predict, given our knowledge about all the variables of car performance (time of day, the weather, road work and so on), is that 1 time in 100, we'll be badly delayed; the other 99 times, we'll arrive at our chosen destination within a range of, say, 40–50 minutes. When we use the knowledge we have and are prepared to think about the things we don't know, then we can take into account that 1 in 100 event and respond accordingly. In our example, that might mean monitoring local traffic radio stations as the "consumer." Or it might mean the highways department—as "supplier"—providing me with early warning through signaling or directing me to alternative routes. We may still miss that 1 in 100 event that could either make or break our business but when we're in what I like to call *Predictive Evaluation* mode, then we will take account of the factors, however unlikely, that could have a tangible impact on performance. This is exactly what air transport carriers strive to do in order to ensure our safety.

From a business perspective, I don't see any reason why companies should not adopt the same broad principles. When they do, it has profound impact. Kevin McGee asserts that *without exception*, business surprises could be anticipated because, to use

McGee's words, "There is always a warning."[2] While McGee's thesis runs the risk of applying hindsight to justify the argument, it has clear merit. When we're working in Predictive Evaluation mode, we anticipate the unexpected. It doesn't catch us off-guard, and we take it as an opportunity to learn. Of course, some companies don't seem to do that and repeat past mistakes.

USING RULES, UNDERSTANDING CORRELATIONS

One of the ways we can mitigate uncertainty is to seek out correlations between events. For example, mobile phone companies have found that if a customer calls (causal event) with the same complaint three times in short succession, there is a fair chance (probability) that he or she will soon switch to another provider (event effect or outcome). In other words, there is a predictable and distinct correlation between a causal event and its outcome. What you need is a method of keeping the customer when the causal event arises. This is where the use of business rules comes in.

Business rules might say that in this scenario don't argue or apologize, just offer to upgrade the phone. If that doesn't work, another rule might kick in and say give the customers the upgraded phone *and* offer them x number of free text messages. The important thing to understand is that you are now imposing rules that may lead to a short-term profits hit but in the long run will keep that customer loyal to your brand and a continuing contributor to bottom-line performance. Before implementing new business rules, you would, of course, figure out which customers you want to keep and run a variety of simulations to assess the impact

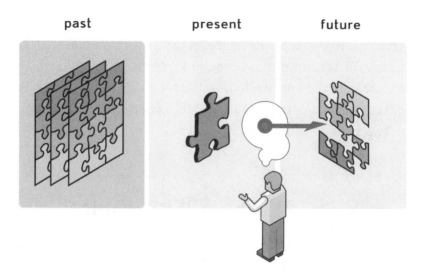

Historical Information. By only having access to historical information for analysis, organizations may be able to tell what happened in the past and have some idea of predictions, but accuracy and timing are highly variable.

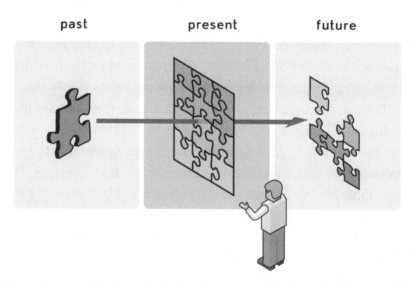

Operational Visibility. By only focusing on operational visibility, an organization loses the context of event correlation based on past performance. Hence, limited ability to take advantage of emerging opportunities.

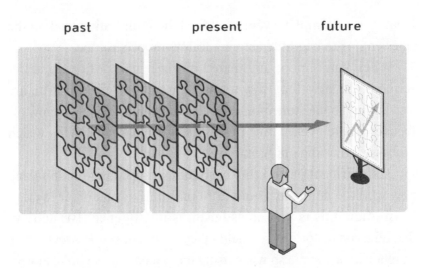

Predictive Business. The organization that not only embraces these two concepts, but also continually draws and updates correlated activities can better compete, lead its market, and avoid surprises.

of making these offers to specific customer segments. Mercenary as this may sound, not every customer is a good, profitable customer. You need to know, for instance, how long customers have been part of your ecosystem, whether they are persistent complainers and if they are tasked with managing their sales force's mobile communications technology. In companies that use business rules effectively, different scenarios will have already been hammered out so that your front line people are well equipped to deal with an unfolding situation. It is also important to keep rules up-to-date as conditions change—then, if competitors introduce a new service, you have a fair idea of what the likely impact will be on your customer churn rate.

For those of you who have studied business rules, or potentially implemented business rules as standard operating procedure, I am not talking here about basic rule usage. I mean systems that can identify *new* complex events and feed the information back to the rules engine to begin detecting a follow-on occurrence.

When you impose automated business rules of the kind described, you are a long way toward automated detection. You are also adding to the store of knowledge that helps define just how effective you are in executing processes, as well as identifying which processes to change or promote.

A significant part of this is about measuring and monitoring how well the company is doing in building its customer loyalty. Most often, this is viewed as business intelligence (BI) activity that relies on historical data held in data warehouses. However, data warehouses are static so when using these techniques you're always running the risk of not knowing what events are impacting current transactions. In other words, you're not maximizing the opportunity to minimize risk. Remember that what we're trying to do is augment our past understanding of customer behavior with current events to discover behavior *predictors* at the time events are occurring.

Patricia Seybold, a well-known consultant who specializes in e-business, expresses it this way:

> Customer value analytics give you the baseline. But they won't tell you how well you're doing in meeting customers' perceived needs. For that, you'll want to add in a way to measure the Quality of Customer Experience (QCE) and to *correlate* it with customer profitability and loyalty. We believe that customer satisfaction and customer loyalty surveys will only give you a rear-view mirror view of QCE. In order to *proactively* manage the experience you deliver for each customer segment, you'll need to add operational metrics that let you monitor, in near *real time*, how you're doing on the particular issues that matter the most to customers in each customer segment and for each of the key Customer Scenarios in each segment.[3] (Emphasis added.)

Seybold asserts it is doable. "For the first time in the history of business, it's now possible to monitor many key business processes end-to-end in near real time. By focusing on the customer scenarios that your customers care about, you can distribute critical, actionable information to the employees and partners who can take immediate steps to improve the quality of the customer experience," says Seybold.[4] At TIBCO, we refer to this as business activity monitoring (BAM), where sensors in the environment trigger alerts to events that require attention.

In the retail industry, companies would like to transmit event information—that is, the customer's response to an offer—to demand-driven manufacturing operations, which then pull products and services from suppliers and business partners to fulfill orders. They want to do this in a real-time environment. Similarly, in the financial services industry, marketing organizations might use customer data to inform business rules management software. In turn, rules engines manage the automated logic behind the modification of marketing and sales campaigns.

A classic example would be the management and execution of new service additions for high-wealth customers. Of course, you need to test whether your new offering is likely to attract fresh funds, but if you are serious about measuring effectiveness, you will closely monitor the campaign as it's playing out. Without rules and process automation, the time and effort required to repeatedly query the data through business intelligence tools would be prohibitive. However, combining rules with the ability to capture small amounts of relevant data generates massive cost savings and compresses the time line between recognizing customer behavior and responding appropriately. This is predictive customer relationship management in action. It combines the real-time execution of rules with fresh data, allowing you to align performance to business goals.

Harrah's Loyal Customers

Gary Loveman, CEO of Harrah's Entertainment Inc., has spent the last seven years transforming the company. Since Loveman joined Harrah's as chief operating officer in 1998, the company has made several large acquisitions including the recent $9.4 billion purchase of Caesars, to become the world's largest casino gaming company with returns on investments that are significantly higher than those of its competitors.

The centerpiece of Loveman's strategy to maximize Harrah's financial performance is the "Total Rewards Card" customer loyalty program, which collects copious amounts of data on customers. Prior to the acquisition of Caesars, Harrah's had an estimated 27 million cardholders in its database.[1] With the addition of Caesars' customers, the total is close to 40 million.[2]

Every time cardholders enter a Harrah's casino, they swipe their card to use slot machines, hand it to a manager to play a game or give it to the cashier to get drinks, meals or hotel rooms.

Harrah's has an extraordinarily detailed view of nearly 80 percent of the customers who gamble at its more than 40 locations: the denomination of their wagering, whether they won or lost, whether they stayed at a Harrah's hotel, what they ate and drank, whether they redeemed a direct mail offer, and if their spouses were with them. The company also knows which of Harrah's casinos they frequent and what games they played. If they were playing the slot machines (which constitute 80 percent of Harrah's revenues), the company even knows how many times they pulled the handle per minute.

All of this real-time data is correlated with historical data (on this customer and his or her peers) to determine what kinds of promotions or special offers will appeal to each customer.

Loveman established a four-tiered reward program, based on the gaming preferences of each group of players. The Seven Stars card is at the top, followed by Diamond, Platinum, and Gold cards. These cards have real meaning and kudos. Customers are given "aspirational incentives" to move up the food chain . . . literally. Take the casino's buffet, for instance. If you have a Seven Stars card you never wait in line for food. If you have Diamond, you might wait a short while. But if you have Gold, you are going to wait in line. "What I wanted," Loveman told me, "was for people standing in the Gold card line to look over at the Seven Stars cardholder being immediately seated, and say, "Gee, if I had one of those cards, I wouldn't be waiting. What do I have to do to get one of those cards?"

The same goes for parking. "If you pull into Harrah's valet parking in New Orleans on a Saturday night and you have a Seven Stars card, you will be valet-parked for free, guaranteed," said Loveman. "You pull in with a Gold card, valet parking is full."

Since the Total Rewards program was introduced, Harrah's estimates it has increased its share of customers' gambling budgets from 36 percent to 43 percent.[3]

Harrah's predictive system has financial impact beyond its casinos. For instance, it has helped fill more hotel rooms at more profitable prices. Increasing the "yield" from hotel properties is one of the primary goals of the Caesars acquisition, Loveman said during a recent conference call with analysts.[4]

The results of Harrah's transformation speak for themselves. In 2004, it was estimated that 75 percent of Harrah's revenue was driven by its loyalty programs.[5] In the same year, Harrah's market capitalization surpassed $7.5 billion, up from approximately $2 billion in 1998.[6] Its 2004 revenues were a record $4.5 billion and net income was $367.7 million—another record.[7]

WINNERS AND LOSERS

You can get pretty inventive about this. Say you are running a national promotion. You are collecting data about how well the promotion is going in different time zones while also making small adjustments to product distribution to optimize fulfillment in each region. But what do you do if a new and unanticipated event occurs that changes the game, and, all of a sudden, you start to see stock wiped out in a particular area? Can you arrange rerouting of goods that are in transit to keep the shelves stocked? What business rules will you apply to help smooth out the demand patterns that are emerging?

For a real-life example of a business turning on a dime to address unexpected changes in demand, look at how Wal-Mart dealt with the impact of Hurricane Frances in Florida in 2004. As soon as the hurricane warning was issued, Wal-Mart's promotions machine revved up. Using information it gathered about spending patterns three weeks earlier (when Hurricane Charlie hit), Wal-Mart was able to predict the likely sales of beer and Pop-Tarts. It then made sure there were plenty of these products available to Floridians before Frances made landfall. In what has now become the stuff of retailing legend, Wal-Mart used its knowledge of customer behavior in these special circumstances to figure out what it had to do and how its processes needed adjustment. The company then applied rules to ensure that its Florida stores could adequately cope with demand. Wal-Mart turned a potential business disruption into a business opportunity.[5]

BUSINESS PROCESS, THE SECRET SAUCE

Business processes play a pivotal role in prediction but this does not mean that applications designed to automate specific business processes will lead the way to Predictive Business. Often the opposite is true because business process applications serve only to eliminate administrative inefficiency. While this may reduce costs, these

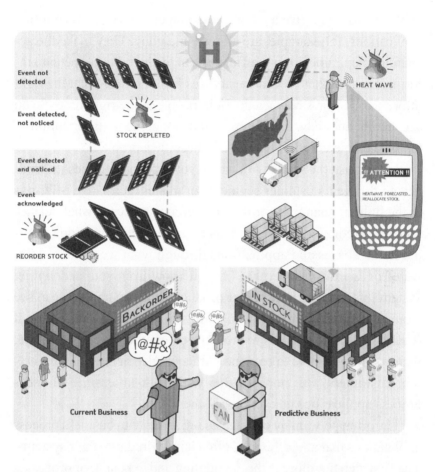

Event Detection & Becoming Proactive. Two retailers in a region may both observe similar threats and opportunities. In the case of one retailer, it fails to understand the dynamic relationship between increased heat, support for localized buying trends and negative customer impact—by not having enough stock on hand to fill demands. The second company has a better understanding of dynamic demand and is able to correlate rising temperatures to not just fill demand, but also balance resources. It identifies the specific retail locations with declining demand and reallocates appropriately to those locations with increasing demand. The result is a DOUBLE WIN—able to service its customers, and service its competitor's unhappy customers.

applications don't give a business a competitive edge. Accounting applications, for example, are all well and good. They make the accounting department more efficient. But they tend to perpetuate information silos that prevent businesses from ensuring that the right information always reaches the right people at the right time. So an accounting anomaly, for example, may not come to the attention of top management until it has already become a problem.

In contrast, the speed with which your company prices its products to different customer segments or makes alternative offerings in the light of changing competitive circumstances is what defines you as a Predictive Business. This requires the integration of corporate databases and applications through what we call "middleware" or "software superglue." If you know from your accounting system that sales of a particular product are down and you can see from the red flags in your customer relationship management (CRM) system that this is related to a competitor's actions in Asia, then you may be able to respond with a quick pricing change to retain customers. But none of this will work unless all business process applications talk to one another.

Unfortunately, many companies are stuck with business process applications that are inflexible, often hard-wired into their systems. The first step therefore is the decoupling and exposing of processes so that they can become "service-centric" in the context of changing conditions. In other words, it is vital to make every database and application available to all parts of a company's business on an as-needed basis.

Decoupling processes has several key benefits:

- Processes can be consumed on an as-needed basis so that they become independent of the function they are serving.

- Having processes available as consumables allows you to reassemble them into new processes at will.

- There is a significant cost savings in IT development because processes are much easier to maintain and deploy when they have been broken down into discrete pieces.

- The company is no longer constrained in its ability to adapt to change. In fact, process shifts from being a potential inhibitor to an enabler of change.

THE PLACE OF BUSINESS PROCESS MANAGEMENT

Yet decoupling business processes is only the start of what needs to be done. Orchestrating processes across the company, its customers and suppliers is the next step and a primary goal for Predictive Business. This is achieved through business process management.

To understand what business process management (BPM) means in the context of *The Power to Predict*, we need some workable definitions. Aberdeen Group says, "BPM is about the reality that business processes are complex, dynamic and intertwined throughout an organization—and, beyond the firewall, to its partners and customers. To effectively automate and manage cross-functional processes requires a new approach and supporting tools that reflect this reality—BPM is that approach. BPM allows processes to be modeled and then dynamically maintained as business requirements are refined or modified, in light of new information on how users work or changing business needs."[6]

So BPM is about bringing order to those processes that distinguish the way you do business—your secret sauce for success. Unfortunately, while many companies understand what their processes contribute to their success, few have documented those processes, let alone determined whether they represent best practices. In the predictive world, this represents a significant problem. If there are undocumented, poorly understood processes, how can a company effectively plan and change its business model? How can the company know whether the processes that have worked well to-date will continue to work if there is a change in the environment? I suggest that figuring this out without BPM is close to impossible.

BPM enables businesses to replace or amend outmoded processes so that the new process slides into place at the point it is required. I will not deny that decoupling, exposing and orchestrating business processes is hardly a trivial task. But the payoff can be enormous.

THE $3 TRILLION OPPORTUNITY

In November 2004, AMR Research declared that it had identified "$488 billion in untapped annual operating margin available to U.S. manufacturers." Businesses could capture their share of that jackpot by adopting best practices in their Internet-enabled supply chains, the analysts said, noting that the $488 billion figure is roughly equivalent to the amount lost after the dot-com bust in 2000–2001.[7] And if that doesn't grab your attention then consider this—according to the same research, companies that embrace demand-driven supply networks:

Have a 5 percent higher profit margin

Deliver up to 10 percent more perfect orders, which in turn increase customer satisfaction and retention

Decrease cash-to-cash cycle times by 35 percent

AMR believes that $3 trillion is locked up in U.S. and European inventories.[8] BPM is about releasing that to shareholders. It is difficult to imagine how the whole of this amount will be released, but the best performers will strive toward getting their slice of this extraordinary mountain of waste.

HOW CAN I APPLY THESE NEW PREDICTIVE PRINCIPLES TO MY BUSINESS?

The Harrah's sidebar in this chapter represents an industry-leading example of predictive business deployments. Today, we are just beginning to see companies using business process management to orchestrate a wide range of business services and act on information provided by business analytics.

In the next few chapters, I will review various industry drivers-in-motion that represent early signs of Predictive Business solutions. Later, I will review what you need to do to deploy a predictive solution and find new opportunities for your business.

EXCELLENCE IN
FINANCIAL SERVICES

FOLLOW THE MONEY

Where is the smart money going? This is usually the best way to identify cutting-edge trends in the financial markets and today is no exception. Following the smart money also provides us with a strong
indicator of technology trends; in financial services, Predictive Business will have a wide variety and high volume of uses.

Today's top buzzword among financial industry insiders is "algorithmic trading." It is an approach to automated trading using com-
puter-managed instructions to maximize the advantages of big money
managers. In the world of algorithmic trading, milliseconds count
and real-time data is really real!

Let us suppose, for example, that a certain mutual fund manager
decides to sell 12 million shares of General Motors stock. (I am not
suggesting that this is a smart move, but it serves to explain the
process.) In the old days, the money manager would call a broker and

agree upon a deal. The broker would then unload the stock, hoping to sell for a higher price.

This was feasible when market information moved slowly and potential buyers were not aware that the broker was flooding the market with GM stock. But today any potential buyer, including the amateur day trader, has almost real-time market information, so the broker's sales are more likely to drive the stock price down as supply outpaces demand.

In algorithmic trading, the sell-off process is automated. A program automatically sells those GM shares in small lots, while monitoring the movement of the share price and timing and adjusting offers accordingly. Algorithmic trading now accounts for about 25 percent of all equity trading volume.[1]

The critical element of algorithmic trading is real-time information. If the trading program knows the latest price just a few fractions of a second before the potential buyer, there is money to be made. So the amateur trader, or even the professional but less tech-savvy trader, is at a disadvantage because he or she does not have the very latest—down to the millisecond—market information.

Algorithmic trading is driving market data message volumes through the roof as programs automatically seek and send data. Over the past three years, market data volumes have risen by 1,750 percent, according to ComStock, a market data supplier. The volume of messages more than doubled in the 12 months ending June 2005, and was projected to continue growing exponentially.[2]

The Options Price Reporting Authority (OPRA), which aggregates all the quotes and trades from the options exchanges, estimates that peak rates will reach 149,000 messages per second by January 2006, more than seven times the 20,378 messages per second it reached in February 2004.[3]

This is placing pressure on investment banks, exchanges and electronic communications networks to upgrade their market data infrastructures as the link between speed and distribution of real-time data becomes critical to profits. In a recent report, Robert Iati of the Tabb Group predicted that, "The emergence of advanced electronic trading, which hinges on real-time analysis of market information as a driver of trading strategies, will force firms to aggressively improve their data infrastructures."[4] Program trading is driving this trend. According to the Tabb Group, it accounted for 20 percent of New York Stock Exchange volume in 2002 and jumped up to 70 percent of the exchange's volume in 2004.[5]

REAL TIME AT THE SPEED OF LIGHT

There are two ways to reduce network latency. One is to increase bandwidth, and financial services companies have already done that. The other approach is to shorten the physical distance between a trader's computers and the exchange because ultimately, no matter how fast data travels, it will take longer to travel farther.

Already INET, Archipelago, and NASDAQ are offering co-location services that enable clients to shave milliseconds off whatever time it may take to send a message from their computers to the market computers.

The next step in algorithmic trading is to test strategies against historical data and change them on the fly. This is the cutting edge of predictive technology and it is already happening.

FAST FLOWING DATA

Liquidnet, which runs a leading and rapidly growing alternative trading system (ATS), allows large money management and investment advisory firms to execute trades directly, among themselves and bypassing exchanges. Formed in 2001, Liquidnet set out to create a network of like-minded, large investors who could trade very large blocks of stock directly with each other. Through Liquidnet, institutions also bypass the typical intermediary broker and dramatically reduce transaction costs. Their trades also occur with complete anonymity, which minimizes the market impact often caused by large trading activities.

Since its launch four years ago, Liquidnet has handled U.S. equity trades with a total value of $351 billion and an average value per trade of over $1 million.[6] Given the massive volume of time-sensitive and confidential information it handles, the Liquidnet system requires very high bandwidth, message throughput and security. Real-time capabilities are also essential so that new trading opportunities can be presented to all members at the same time.

"To be fair to all of our members, we needed to make sure we could present liquidity to all members at the same time when a new member came on board with a lot of liquidity to present," says Seth Merrin, CEO of Liquidnet.[7] The trading system links into fund managers' order management systems to see what trades they want to make and then goes out into the market to find suitable matches.

As I have previously described, TIBCO got its start in integrating Wall Street trading floors. This revolutionized the stock market and paved the way for true real-time operations. By today's standards, those systems we developed in the 1990s were primitive, but they laid the groundwork for future developments.

Today, we are a primary provider of messaging software to companies such as Liquidnet that are in the forefront of real-time trading.

A CHANGE OF PACE

Predictive technologies clearly have their place in the rarefied world of programmed trading. But do they have any relevance for the financial services used by the average man in the street?

The answer is "yes," but not in the way that you might imagine. In the retail banking industry, the top issues are customer acquisition and customer retention. Customer acquisition tends to boil down to old-fashioned "feet on the street" principles. The banks that have branches in the right places, staffed by people who have been well trained, will win new customers.

A few years ago, many were predicting that e-banking and ATMs would kill off branch banking. However, reports of branch banking's death have been greatly exaggerated. Between 1992 and 2002, the number of FDIC-insured bank branches grew from 62,000 to over 72,000.[8]

Celent reports that the retail banking industry opened five new branches daily throughout 2004. However, the *activities* in bank branches have changed markedly in recent years. According to Celent's research, only 45 percent of branch activities are now transaction-related (deposits, withdrawals, transfers, etc.).[9] Instead, today's bank branches spend more time on sales and service.

While the branches do a good job at attracting new customers, the bigger challenge is to keep those customers. Customer relationship management systems were supposed to take care of this issue, but most banks lack the systems and integration needed to create a "single view of the customer."

Superior customer service and increased customer retention are vital to any financial institution. A study by Reichheld and Sasser published in the *Harvard Business Review* found that some organizations could boost profits by almost 100 percent by retaining just 5 percent more of their customers.[10] Implementing practices that help increase customer retention and customer service is therefore critical to sustaining profitability and competitive advantage.

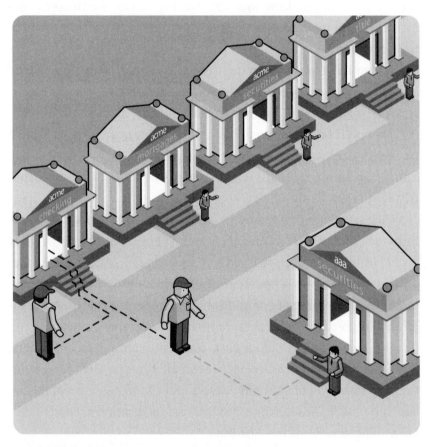

That's My Bank for. . . Customers have many options for financial services. Banks with improper service integration fail to clearly communicate the value of leveraging other offers and waste opportunities daily as customers literally walk into one bank for checking, another for securities, and another for retirement planning.

This is where real-time data can help by enabling retail banks to achieve a much broader and clearer view of their customers. Integrating customer records from every part of a bank's operations and updating them in real time is the only way to ensure that a bank, or any business, can proactively deal with problems. Moreover, it is also the best way for a bank to spot opportunities to expand its relationship with a customer. If, for example, a customer makes a much larger than average deposit, this is a signal for the bank to inquire whether the customer has won the lottery or transferred funds to a checking account in preparation for a large purchase. Perhaps it is time to call that customer to see if he or she may be looking for a loan or investment vehicle, or whether a life change is underway that could create other banking service opportunities.

Another example might be the banking customer who calls to find out the payoff amount on a mortgage. Is he or she considering refinancing through a competitor? It is certainly worth asking the question and making a counteroffer. Or perhaps the customer is selling the property to reinvest the proceeds. That could create another high-value opportunity.

Analysis of real-time data to trigger responses can enhance sales as well as build a more loyal customer base. However, the challenge of "knowing the customer" has been greatly exacerbated by bank mergers and acquisitions. There is an apocryphal story told by industry insiders of a multimillionaire who held a very large investment account with a brokerage that was acquired by a large U.S. bank. As the story goes, this individual became incensed when he was charged $2.50 to withdraw a small amount of cash from one of the bank's ATMs. He called the bank's customer service line to complain but was rebuffed because he did not have a checking account at the bank. The wealthy customer withdrew all

My Bank Makes It Easy. By integrating the operations, practices and redundant processes, organizations can more rapidly deliver value to customers in the form of incentives, consolidated banking and simplified transactions.

of his funds from his brokerage account in disgust. The problem, of course, stemmed from the fact that the bank did not have the "single view of the customer" that is essential to ensure good customer service and retention.

A broader view of customer relationships can uncover even more opportunities. For example, could a different mix of products produce a higher return to both the customer and the bank? Did the customer's address recently change, signaling the need for new or different services? Is the customer regularly using other banks' ATMs, and is there an opportunity for the bank to capture that lost revenue by deploying an ATM of its own?

DO YOU KNOW YOUR BANKER?

Most American consumers have very narrow relationships with their banks. A 2004 study of U.S. households by Forrester Research discovered 38 percent of those with checking accounts had no other products (loans, credit cards, investments, etc.) with their bank. Another 38 percent had just one secondary relationship with their bank. In addition, the research found only 28 percent would consider their bank for future financial products, well below the percentage of households that would buy again from their insurance companies, brokerages or credit unions. Finally, Forrester reported that nearly half of U.S. households ended a banking relationship at least once because they were dissatisfied; of this group, more than a third switched banks two or more times.[11]

"The key to gaining and sustaining organic growth is the seamless integration of all related sales and service capabilities," says Scott Forbes, Accenture managing partner.[12] He points to integration of customer data as the best way to present an accurate view of the customer (including relationship potential) throughout an enterprise. Providing actionable customer insights to an empowered sales force will also enable banks to leverage their sales and service abilities, he adds.

THE FUTURE OF RETAIL BANKING

In Spain, Solbank has established itself as a bank of choice for European expatriates looking for one-stop convenience. A subsidiary of Banco Sabadell, Spain's fourth largest banking group, Solbank appeals directly to the person who is new to the country and plans to own either a holiday or permanent home. The default language for its Web site is English although users can select from Spanish, German, and French. Its branches are concentrated in areas where "expats" like to live, especially in the Costa Blanca and Costa de Sol areas. It continues to expand the branch network as new parts of Spain become popular with expats. Its services are not the most competitive. For example, loan terms are not as generous as those offered by some competitors. But it is convenient. An integral part of its overall service offering is its Prestige Care Club where members can access non-financial services including legal, medical, and translation services. It will even arrange for taxi services, emergency home maintenance, 24-hour veterinary services and flower deliveries. Customers pay for these services based on published scale rates. Again, these are not the best prices one could obtain for these services, but they are convenient. The flipside is that Solbank offers its customers free withdrawals and direct debit payment facilities provided they are prepared to forgo paper statements.

Given that Spain is one of the 21st century's hottest European property markets, attracting billions of dollars of inward investment each year, Solbank is making an extremely attractive play. The success of its approach can be measured by the fact that during 2003 (the last year for which full segment analysis is publicly available), the bank increased the value of assets under management by 31 percent and attracted more than 28,700 new customers.

Solbank is a great example of an institution that has figured out what its target audience wants and has pitched a set of services that make it a highly attractive alternative to a fast-growing niche. It has successfully predicted that offering a range of carefully packaged financial and non-financial services provides a route to spectacular, organic growth.

WHOSE DATA IS IT?

The value of customer data increases exponentially as it is amalgamated to create a single view of the customer. Yet the responsibilities involved in protecting this data also grow and create new challenges. As leading U.S. banks and credit card processors have learned, to their chagrin, the accidental or fraudulent loss of customer data can undermine the trust that is an essential part of any financial institution's relationship with its customers.

The private financial records of tens of thousands of Americans were inadvertently or fraudulently exposed in the first few months of 2005. Incidents ranged from hackers breaking into the computer systems of banks and other financial services companies to the inexplicable loss of end-of-day data tapes that were shipped to data centers without due regard for security.

Yet the same technologies that are driving the collection of customer data can also address the security problems that many now fear. Analysis of real-time and historical data is already widely used in credit card fraud detection. Many of us have firsthand experience of this if we have attempted to make an unusually large purchase using a credit card or used the card abroad for the first time. Any such "unusual" activity is likely to prompt at best a phone call from the card processing company to check that this is not a fraudulent transaction, or at worst an awkward situation when the credit card charge is refused.

U.S. banks have a strong incentive to root out credit card fraud because they are liable for any loss over $50. Unfortunately, the same is not yet true of losses associated with the other types of accounts. In the future, banks and other financial institutions will surely recognize that they must apply the same real-time data analysis now used by credit card processors to other aspects of their business if they are to retain the trust of their customers.

chapter

ANSWERING TELCO'S CALL

IN A 1976 *Saturday Night Live* skit, Lily Tomlin captured American consumers' frustrations with AT&T's long-distance telephone service monopoly. Acting the role of the telephone operator, she dismissed a customer's complaint: "We don't care. We don't have to. We're the Phone Company."

To this day, Tomlin's skit echoes around the Internet and is typically quoted as the antithesis of "customer-centric" business strategy. But it no longer applies to phone companies. Over the past 30 years, the telecommunications sector has been transformed by deregulation and new technologies into an intensely customer-aware industry. AT&T's hubris is history. Today's communications service providers face tough and complex challenges as they work to win new customers and retain the ones they have. Any communications company that doesn't *care* about its customers today doesn't care about staying in business.

Deregulation tore apart former monopolies such as AT&T, but advances in communications technologies have caused even more disruption in the telecoms industry. The emergence of cellular wireless communications in the 1980s, the Internet in the 1990s and later, broadband communications, created many more challenges for "phone companies" and even made that term obsolete. Today, the companies that provide communications services might better be described as networking providers. Tomorrow they might look more like entertainment companies in the consumer market and communications utilities in the enterprise sector. Whatever their moniker, they face stiff competition on many fronts.

In a world where there is plenty of choice, consumers are primarily concerned that service should meet or exceed their expectations. They don't much care how that service gets to them. In the UK and much of Europe, voice service is widely offered as part of a package including cable television and Internet access. Today's American consumers, in contrast, are more likely to pay monthly bills to a local phone company, a long-distance provider, a separate cable television account and yet another provider of Internet access. However, plans by cable giant Comcast to enter the voice market, and by leading telcos such as SBC to deliver television programming, suggest that convergence is getting underway here too. In the future, any network operator with a line into the home can—in theory at least—offer a wide range of services.

In the business arena, companies that used to be geared to data communications are adding voice services to their product offerings, while "telcos" are deeply involved in distributing data and software applications. Virtual private network services, delivered with service guarantees, are competing with the telco offerings. Meanwhile, wireless (mobile) communications have become a vital element of business for both voice and data transmissions.

In short, consumers and businesses now have a wide range of choices and a confusing array of promises and prices. But this is just the beginning.

WHITHER POTS?

A quarter of Western European households will abandon "plain old telephone services" (POTS) by 2010, according to Analysys, a leading telco research and consulting group. Europeans spent more on mobile voice calls in 2004 than they did on landline calls, the researchers found, and they project a steep decline in traditional phone service revenues. "We expect the proportion of mobile-only households to increase to nearly 18 percent in 2010," the researchers said. By 2010, POTS services will account for just 39 percent of spending on residential voice services in Western Europe, they predict.[1]

In the United States, we are playing catch up but a "tipping point" was reached at the end of 2004 when the FCC reported that, for the first time, more Americans were talking on cell phones than on traditional landlines. The report found that from 2003 to 2004, mobile subscribers increased about 15 percent to 181.1 million— more than half of the U.S. population. Meanwhile, landline subscribers grew just 3 percent to 177.9 million.[2]

VoIP

Telcos are now gearing up for a new round of intense competition with the growing popularity of Voice over Internet Protocol (VoIP), a technology that could undermine the pricing structure of the entire industry by eliminating distance as a factor in how much users pay to make a phone call. As Michael Powell, former chairman of the U.S. Federal Communications Commission, said, "I knew it was over when I downloaded Skype. When the inventors of KaZaA are distributing for free a little program that you can use to talk to anybody else, and the quality is fantastic, and it's free—it's over. The world will change now inevitably."[3] For around $20 a month, U.S. residents can buy unlimited national and international VoIP services with most of the features of a "traditional" phone line including voice mail, caller ID and so on. The one significant drawback of VoIP has been difficulty reaching 911 emergency services that use incoming phone numbers to determine the location of callers. This should be rectified by September 2005 by order of the FCC.

These so-called "open" VoIP services link to POTS and mobile networks, providing a viable and cheaper alternative to the services of traditional telcos.

Some 6 million Americans will be using VoIP services by the end of 2005, according to research firm Gartner. and other industry experts predict that group could swell to 40% of the U.S. market by 2009.[4] Traditional telcos are not ignoring the trend. Indeed, several are entering the VoIP market themselves. AT&T, for example, has withdrawn from the traditional residential phone service market, but does offer a consumer VoIP service. SBC has announced plans for VoIP trials in Los Angeles, Dallas, Chicago and San Antonio[5] and other carriers are following suit. In a new twist on VoIP, Sprint has agreed to assist cable TV operator Comcast in getting its VoIP service off the ground.[6]

The picture is similar in Europe where open VoIP services are growing strongly in France, Italy, and Sweden. "The usage of broadband connections for VoIP is at a nascent stage in Western Europe currently, but the scene will change dramatically over the next five years," says Katrina Bond of Analysys. Her research suggests that VoIP could account for 9.6 percent of voice minutes by 2010, but only around 3.6 percent of "voice spend" because VoIP is so much cheaper than traditional phone services.[7]

Extrapolating on the VoIP trend, some industry observers have predicted that landline voice service will eventually be free. "The idea of charging for calls belongs to the last century," says Niklas Zennström, chief executive and co-founder of Skype, a VoIP service that allows users of Skype software to make free calls over the Internet.[8] Skype claims to be signing up 150,000 new users a day and to have 1.4 million paying customers for its SkypeOut service, which enables calls from users' computers to "normal" (landline or wireless) phones and from normal phones to any Skype user's PC.[9]

Speaking at the VON Europe 2005 conference in Stockholm, Zennström caused quite a stir when he predicted that phone companies would have to change their business models. "If you fast forward 10 years all [telcos'] revenue will come from Internet access and none from voice minutes or line rental."[10]

Zennström and others who predict that voice calls over landlines will be free of charge may be overstating the case but certainly, the prospect of POTS becoming "profit-free" is spurring activity and realignment among traditional players in the telco industry.

In a March 2005 Congressional hearing concerning the proposed mergers of AT&T with SBC, MCI with Verizon, and Sprint with Nextel, Verizon chairman and chief executive Ivan Seidenberg noted, "Long distance and local as stand-alone businesses are on their way to obsolescence. . . ."[11] Michael Capellas, MCI chief executive, added ". . . long distance is almost now perceived to be free," because many wireless phone services do not distinguish between local and long-distance calls. "The concept of long distance as a product will cease to exist, whether it is in the consumer market or, frankly in the business market," he testified. "Voice simply becomes a feature on an advanced network."[12]

IPTV

Even as they await regulatory approvals for their respective merger plans, companies such as SBC and Verizon are pouring billions of dollars into broadband fiber networks. SBC, for example, has undertaken a $4 billion network upgrade called Project Lightspeed to provide consumers with the next generation of high-speed data, voice and video services.

"We will deploy an additional 40,000 miles of fiber in our networks—in some cases taking the fiber directly to the premises—enabling a full range of IP services and features. This will deliver bandwidth of 20 to 25 megabits . . . more than four times as fast as our fastest broadband speeds today," said Edward E. Whitacre Jr., SBC chairman and chief executive, speaking at the 2005 International Consumer Electronics Show. He added, "That's more than enough to provide high-definition IPTV, superfast broadband and video on demand—and just about any other application you can think of."[13]

The challenges of delivering content are a future model for network operators around the world as they expand their offerings to include digital delivery of products and services. The IPTV user ordering a movie and the cellular subscriber ordering a plane ticket represent similar transactions and similar complexities.

IPTV in particular, is capturing attention. "You will be able to choose the shows you want to watch, and you will be able to watch them whenever you want to. You will be able to edit shows, choose camera angles during athletic events, use interactive features, and pull up information from the Internet—and much more—all while you are watching a program," Whitacre promised.[14]

"The widespread attention given the many flavors of convergence technologies at the January [2005] Consumer Electronics

Show points to the inevitable marriage of IP and TV. Broadband and video are two of the triple play's three pillars and once these are in place, voice—VoIP—will quickly follow," says Jon Arnold of industry analysts Frost and Sullivan.[15]

The convergence of entertainment with wireless communications is also moving apace, particularly in Asia and Europe where superior digital wireless networks have spurred data wireless services ranging from text messaging via mobile phones, to widespread "m-commerce" and downloading of games and video, to the latest generation of converged devices that incorporate mobile phones.

"All kinds of traffic—phone calls, e-mail messages, and even cable television—will travel over a single network based on Internet protocols. And we'll access all that information through devices that don't really resemble the traditional gadgets we now use,"[16] *Fortune's* Stephanie Mehta predicts.

For network operators, the new consumer battlefield is content, including sports scores, games, news and entertainment, distributed over wireless networks. This has plunged telcos into the unfamiliar arena of content sourcing and the complexities of revenue sharing, as they pay revenues to content producers as well as fees to advertisers. Knowing the customer has become an essential element of success because, like TV networks, the phone companies must deliver desirable content.

BUSINESS SLAs

In the business world, quality of service is of paramount importance. Most large corporate clients demand a service level agreement (SLA) which details the level of service the telco guarantees to provide. Service standards have long been the norm, but until recently they were mostly of the "one size fits all" variety and were loosely enforced. Competition has lead to more stringent application of SLAs, and customers are beginning to demand services tailored to their specific requirements. This might mean, for example, that the network operator has to meet a customer's peak demand between 8 A.M. and 9 A.M., making the customer's needs a top priority during those hours. Rather than responding to outages within a period specified in an SLA, operators are now applying predictive techniques to preempt and resolve problems before the customer is affected.

Let's say, for example, that a bank has signed a premium SLA contract with the service provider for 98 percent availability of broadband services. The account manager and operations managers need instant notification if this SLA may be in jeopardy, and they need to know *before* it has been violated. This can be achieved by monitoring the real-time transaction report stream and comparing it to performance objectives or rules established for that customer's service. By comparing patterns of performance, we can extrapolate trends and predict within a very short time frame that problems will occur if a current trend continues. This condition might trigger an automated "fix," perhaps the diversion of traffic to an alternative route or alerting the operations manager to intervene.

SERVICE CONVERGENCE

With basic connectivity rapidly commoditizing and aggressive challengers entering the field, telecom providers have had to quickly transform business models to deliver integrated services and rich content. Vertically integrated monopolies are becoming one piece in a much larger value web involving content, equipment, software, and other third-party service providers. Having worked with some of the largest telecommunications firms in the world including KPN, Deutsche Telekom, Virgin Mobile, Vodafone, Cingular,

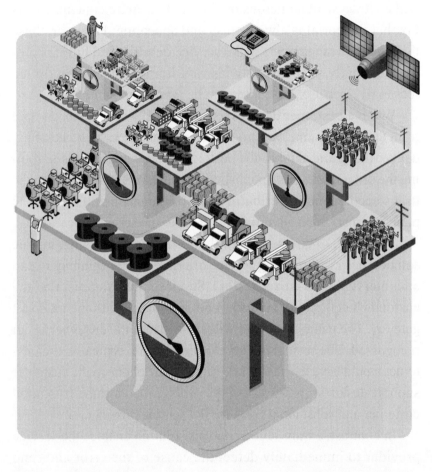

Service Level Balancing Act. Every day, managers make decisions based on demands, resources, threats and opportunities. The larger the organization, the more complex the relationship between other groups, departments and business units. Synchronization is key as latencies in identification and action can create a snowball effect impacting the furthest reaches of an organization.

and many others, we have seen tremendous strides in adapting to this new service deployment technique.

Without getting into the specifics of any one provider, let's take an example like a mobile portal, which provides consumers with games, ring tones, sports and news available for download. A telco will contract with numerous publishers to acquire content, ensuring that the portal is always fresh and appealing. However, these third-party arrangements make service delivery and billing complex. Similarly, payment methods vary from monthly subscription fees to pay-per-use, depending on the type of content.

When a customer decides to download, for instance, a game from the portal, numerous processes must take place to successfully deliver that game and bill the customer. These might include routing the order to the game publisher, recording the transaction on the user's account, and distributing part of the payment to the game publisher, part to an advertiser and part to the service operator.

There are, of course, lots of things that can go wrong, but the solution lies in monitoring service offerings from beginning to end and intervening to correct errors. Suppose, for example, that the customer's cell phone number is not registered with the payment gateway. The game download will fail because the customer is not recognized. The results are all too predictable: typically, the customer would have to spend a long time on the phone to the customer support desk trying to resolve the problem, creating a frustrated customer and substantial costs for the service provider.

In contrast, a transaction analysis solution enables the service provider to immediately detect the cause of the error and send an appropriate text message to the customer—a message asking whether he or she is registered on the micro-payment gateway. When the customer replies and registration is confirmed, a second text message, or SMS (short message service), incorporating download instructions can be sent to his or her cell phone. The customer can then complete the transaction, download the game and pay for it.

In addition, the service provider could have included a promotional offer in the resolution message, such as "buy 10 games for a discount of 20 percent." At this point, the end user is paying attention to the service provider's messages and is more likely to accept this offer than a standard, unsolicited promotion.

An added benefit of this approach is that it may highlight a systemic problem. Perhaps new subscribers are not being registered with the payment gateway fast enough, or there is some other problem that is preventing registration. If a pattern of transaction problems can be identified, action can be taken to resolve the issue.

There will be times, of course, when the problem cannot be resolved so easily. But the costs and frustrations can be minimized by real-time information monitoring and exception management.

All information about every single user transaction is collected, correlated and presented as needed to the customer service and/or support operations. Whenever a user complains or inquires about a particular service or transaction, the call center will immediately know that the transaction actually happened, the outcome and status of the transaction and, in case of a failure, the reason for the failure.

END-TO-END VISIBILITY

The real-time data gathered in the process of monitoring transactions provides companies with a wealth of information about customers. In the past, telcos could identify customers as big spenders and might analyze their call patterns to identify opportunities to sell new calling packages, but they had very little information beyond this. Now telcos will need to know a lot more:

What products are most popular with their customers?

What is the uptake and usage of a particular service over time, by geography or demography?

How much revenue is generated by service type/geography/demography over time?

Which third-party content providers are living up to service quality agreements?

In addition, transaction monitoring presents a multitude of possibilities for interacting with the customer and driving business decisions in real time. This is vital because in a rapidly changing environment, telcos must be extremely agile.

They have to be flexible in mixing and matching services, in turning on and off services and in coordinating business activities behind those services. They must also be able to track customers' tastes in content and manage relationships with third-party content providers. Real-time transaction data will be essential as the role of the telco shifts from being a communications utility to a content retailer.

SBC VERSUS COMCAST

As this is written, a marketing battle is gearing up in the San Francisco Bay Area between SBC, the dominant telco, and Comcast, the nation's largest cable TV provider. Both are about to launch plans to invade each other's territory. This battle is, in microcosm, one that has already played out or soon will in many other parts of the world.

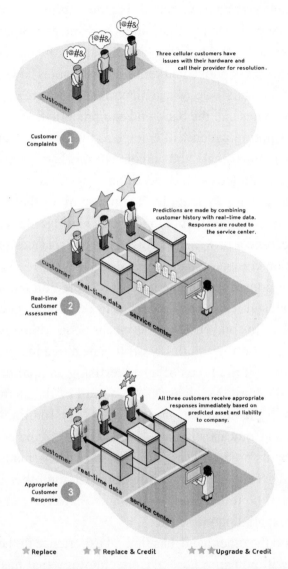

Three cellular customers have issues with their hardware and call their provider for resolution.

Customer Complaints 1

customer

Predictions are made by combining customer history with real-time data. Responses are routed to the service center.

Real-time Customer Assessment 2

customer   real-time data   service center

All three customers receive appropriate responses immediately based on predicted asset and liability to company.

Appropriate Customer Response 3

customer   real-time data   service center

★ Replace   ★★ Replace & Credit   ★★★ Upgrade & Credit

Recognizing & Adjusting Service to Meet Customer Needs. Three customers calling for service may have very similar problems, but should they be treated the same? One might be a long-time customer, another may have only been a customer for a couple of months, but has spent significantly, and the other customer might be calling about the same problem for a third time. Correlating customers' usage patterns with current conditions will enable customer service to maximize the effectiveness of the unique, tailored response.

The cable company, Comcast, is planning to offer phone service. The phone company, SBC, aims to displace Comcast in television. Both will offer bundled broadband Internet access. SBC is also in the wireless phone market. Both companies have pluses and minuses in terms of the physical plants that they have in place—the "wires" to homes and the back-end equipment—that may be critical in determining which will emerge as the Bay Area victor.

Yet on a global scale, the outcome of this battle between cable companies and telcos will depend more upon the abilities of the various combatants to adapt to the opportunities that new broadband communications technologies are creating. Is it easier for a telco to become a provider of entertainment services or for a cable television company to offer voice services?

From a consumer perspective, the cable companies (in the United States at least) have a barrier to overcome. Their reputation for reliability and customer service is poor. Although Comcast has made great efforts to throw off this negative image, going so far as to make it the focus of an advertising campaign, first impressions die hard. Much as AT&T, for all of the changes it has made, is still the "Phone Company" that Lily Tomlin derided 30 years ago, so Comcast still carries the baggage of the poor reputation held by its predecessors in the cable industry (many of which it acquired). So the challenge for Comcast and other U.S. cable services will be to persuade consumers that they can rely upon them for essential phone services.

SBC, on the other hand, has limited experience in the TV business and will be using new IPTV technology that has yet to be proven on a large scale. "The Bells are being forced to respond [to competition from cable TV companies]. But they don't have a real video product yet and fiber optics will take awhile because of labor, technology and regulatory and capital issues," Aryeh Bourkoff of UBS told the *San Francisco Chronicle*.[17]

Another important factor in this and other cable-versus-telco battles will be the abilities of these companies to "know the customer." Like Harrah's and Wal-Mart and other leaders in consumer industries, they will need to be able to monitor consumer tastes in real time and then predict what TV programming, what mixes of bundled services and what pricing will win them new customers.

WHAT NEXT FOR TELCOS?

At a time of intense competitive pressure and relentless customer churn, the ability of telcos to demonstrate exemplary customer service is critical. The effectiveness with which they can maintain service quality has a direct impact on their abilities to attract new customers and maximize revenues from existing customers. Execution and optimization will also impact the bottom line.

Traditional telcos are racing to find new sources of revenue as POTS are displaced by mobile and VoIP calls and cable TV operators muscle their way into the phone market. Telcos must now reinvent themselves. Proactively managing complexity in real time will be critical.

TRANSPORTATION AND LOGISTICS— IMPROVING DELIVERY

GLOBALIZATION OF TRADE is creating increased demand for both transportation and logistics organizations. The scale of growth is staggering. According to the Department of Transportation, freight activity across the continental United States is expected to rise from 15 billion tons in 1998 to 25 billion tons by 2020,[1] a two-thirds increase.

International shipping is also growing fast, driven by the rise of offshoring. In particular, offshore manufacturing and assembly has necessitated shipping between distant locations, bringing the right goods to the right locations at the right times and doing it efficiently and cheaply. The raw materials used to build a product may be produced in one country, assembled in another and finally marketed to consumers in many other parts of the world.

Depending on the industry sector, supply chain logistics costs range from 5 to 50 percent of a product's delivered cost.[2] Minimizing supply chain costs has therefore become a high priority for many industries. The Performance Measurement Group, a supply chain consultancy, finds a strong correlation between supply chain best practices and financial performance.[3]

Logistics consultant Carla Reed underscores this point in her own research, noting that best-practice supply chains operate with up to 50 percent lower inventory cost than the median for an industry sector. Reed finds reducing inventory is a key issue in supply chain management and the biggest cause of inventory stockpiling is uncertainty: "The key to managing this uncertainty is accurate and real-time information. As such, the flow of information, concurrent with the flow of goods and performance of services, provides the mechanism to manage the various links in the supply chain."[4]

FEDEX—A LOGISTICS POSTER CHILD

It's not often a business name becomes part of the collective psyche but FedEx is an exception. When someone promises to send over a package by express courier, he or she is likely to say, "I'll FedEx it." Over the years, the FedEx name has become synonymous with reliable delivery of everything from critical business documents to high-value components for the tech industry and lifesaving blood plasma. The FedEx name has also come to represent customers' ability to quickly and easily track the location of a package in transit.

Maintaining the high standards that FedEx has come to stand for, as well as enhancing customer service across 220 countries and 375 airports around the globe, is the job of Rob Carter, executive vice president and chief information officer.[5] IT investment

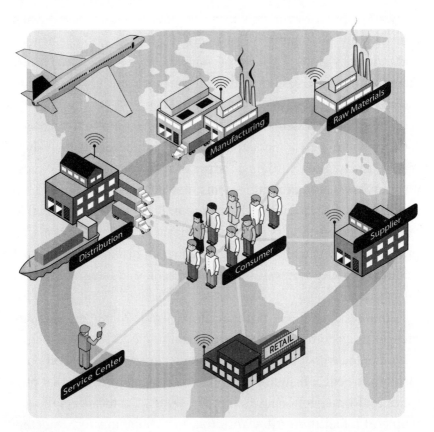

Eager Network. The eager network trumps conventional wisdom that organizations create value by strictly following a pre-determined, plan-source-make-deliver model. The eager network places the consumer at the center to rapidly anticipate needs and proactively coordinate the delivery of products and services.

at FedEx is driven by customer requirements, he explains. "The strategic focus on technology is about the customer. How can we make the customer happier and more effective in their business by providing information they need to literally grow revenue?"[6]

FedEx is an aggressive user of new technology. Rather than wait for a particular technology to mature, FedEx prefers to be an early adopter. However, new technology is only introduced when the company can justify the cost with improved customer benefit and efficiency gains. This approach has allowed it to develop an efficient global ecosystem in which partners and customers are viewed as integral parts of what FedEx does.

The symbiosis stems from the now famous track and trace systems that permit customers to determine the progress of their shipments. Today, FedEx offers an array of additional tools that meet a variety of customer requirements. For instance, its Global Ship Manager is a combination hardware and software solution that high volume customers integrate with their existing systems, to provide end users with a tracking mechanism inside their merchant trading accounts. In turn, FedEx offers back-end integration to its own systems.

Another example is FedEx's Global Trade Manager. This service helps customers reduce the amount of cargo stranded in customs due to errors in filing international paperwork. The company also offers FedEx Insight—a reverse tracking application that provides real-time, actionable shipment status. Carter offers the example of a facility in New York that tests bone marrow to determine the viability for transplant matches. "We found this testing lab did not know how many of these kinds of samples they would get in a day, nor did they know how many samples to expect to receive from various locations. When they used Insight and acquired information about doctors' offices and facilities that had sent them material via FedEx, by midnight they would know how many extracts to expect the next day, and they could plan according[ly]."[7]

FedEx is taking a measured approach to the introduction of radio frequency identification (RFID) technology. As Carter explains, "The technology associated with reading and gathering the information from RFID is probably about one-third of the battle. Most of what needs to happen in logistics information systems involves managing and utilizing that information once you have it."[8]

Currently, FedEx collects most of its logistics and tracking information using bar codes and that is not going to change overnight. However, the company has been quietly experimenting with different RFID applications for some years. FedEx tracks movements of its 30,000 tractor trailers and trucks in and out of FedEx's yards using RFID tags. RFID also helps FedEx to route trucks automatically to a package's end-point location, without necessarily having to touch every piece of freight in dock operations.

In the future, FedEx sees RFID tags in "high velocity" shipments of perishable goods. RFID's ability to handle dynamic information would, for example, make it valuable in raising an alarm if meat and blood products are exposed to rising temperatures. The RFID tag could send an alert to an appropriate person for appropriate action before the product is spoiled.

It is apparent that distributing real-time information and using applications that respond to events differentiates FedEx from its competition. And from the FedEx perspective, it doesn't matter whether the package is at rest or in motion—information about that package has customer value. Customers like to feel they're in control and FedEx delivers on that requirement. But the company goes a lot further than putting track and trace into customers' hands. For example, its customs management helps ensure that customers pay the correct amount of duty by providing detailed and accurate information about the products that are arriving or being shipped. Carter says:

> Our advantage is that we do all of that electronically, including all the documentation and all the forms, so it arrives prior to the arrival of the aircraft and the physical goods. And we install the technology for customs authorities around the world. We give them the ability to look at the inbound manifest of shipments.

Ultimately, there are specific business rules and regulatory rules that apply and that is where IT can be applied flexibly in different markets and in different settings, as opposed to tangling all of that up in a code base.[9]

In short, FedEx works toward making life as easy as possible for everyone in the logistics value chain.

SOUTHWEST AIRLINES— BUCKING TRENDS

"Welcome to San Jose International Airport. Please check the seat pockets in front of you." For frequent air travelers, the announcement is all too familiar and all too easily ignored. But the Southwest Airlines flight attendant goes on to say, "And if you are missing any valuable items when you deplane, you will find them tomorrow morning on eBay!"

This is typical of Southwest's corporate humor and one of many things that sets this airline apart from its more traditional peers. Another is its financial performance. Even as many other U.S. airlines struggle to stay aloft, Southwest has recorded its 57th consecutive profitable quarter in July 2005.[10] It is now one of the largest airlines in the United States and is in better financial health than almost any other. What is more, Southwest has achieved this by breaking with conventional airline passenger wisdom, pioneering a no-frills approach with no seat assignments and no fancy food. Flight attendants wear shorts or slacks. There is no first class cabin and no coddling of passengers before or during the flight. To catch a Southwest flight, you may have to find your way to the secondary airports serving major metropolitan areas. Yet in contrast to most budget airlines, Southwest gives all passengers leather seats with more legroom than average. And its fares, of course, are typically much lower than those of its competitors.

Southwest also has its own unique approach to the use of technology. The airline has been a leader in front end, self-service booking (via its Web site) and advance check-in (on the Web as well as at electronic kiosks in airports). But until recently, Southwest has been a laggard in terms of IT support for its operations.

"In many ways, our technology is ahead, but technology at our airports has been behind," Gary Kelly, Southwest CEO, acknowledges. Now, "throughout our organization—finance, back office, managing flight crews, maintenance crews at hangars—we're employing more and more technology tools."[11]

Southwest's heightened interest in technology has been born of necessity. The airline, which currently carries 70 million travelers per year, expects 10 percent annual growth over the next two years. Southwest also expects to add 59 aircraft to its 420-plane fleet.[12] With growth has come complexity and Southwest is now playing catch-up. In fact, Southwest is leaping from behind the times to using real-time data. And it's paying off. Since September of 2004, Southwest has reduced by as much as 15 percent the time that planes undergoing scheduled maintenance are out of service.[13]

For each of Southwest's nearly 3,000 daily flights,[14] an enormous amount of data is collected including flight route, fuel requirements and weather information. But the airline's flight management system—Southwest Integrated Flight Tracking system (SWIFT), developed in-house—could not be scaled to keep pace with growth. What was needed was a real-time messaging tool to ensure that the most up-to-date information could be delivered to the right people at the right time.

The new system manages literally thousands of FAA weather messages and delivers them immediately to the appropriate sub-

scribers. Users who need the information get it as soon as it becomes available, and they're not swamped with irrelevant data.
The result is that Southwest is now well positioned to keep customers informed and proactively manage the inevitable gate
changes and personnel redeployments when weather conditions
demand.

Southwest is just beginning to reap the benefits of real-time
operation. "It has been a real eye-opening experience," says Kevin
Dirks, Southwest systems engineer. "We are continually discover-
ing new applications [for real-time messaging]."[15]

LIGHT-ASSET LOGISTICS

In the logistics industry, there are two kinds of players: those that
own the vehicles and airplanes and equipment used to transport
goods around the world, and those that partner with the truckers
and airlines and shippers. The latter are known as "asset-light" logistics providers; they would seem to be at a huge disadvantage
compared to asset-intensive operations such as FedEx, because
they don't own the networks over which they operate. This means
they don't have control over many of the factors that may impact
their ability to ensure customer satisfaction. However, this is not
universally true.

UTi is an international asset-light supply chain management
company providing air and ocean freight forwarding, contract logistics, customs brokerage, and other logistics-related services. In
2002, UTi announced its NextLeap strategy, a multi-year project
designed to enable the company to grow rapidly, increase revenues
and improve margins.[16]

A central component of that strategy has been the implementation of a comprehensive integration program designed to im-

The Right Information to the Right Person at the Right Time. The absence of timely and contextual information can create frustration, wasted time and effort. Yet, the ability to provide proactive information can help customers with time management and ease tension.

prove business agility and visibility into compartmentalized business operations—such as warehousing, distribution and freight forwarding. This integration allowed UTi's customers to track their goods in transit around the globe.

The improved tracking capabilities have contributed to improved customer service and increased revenue growth as well as operational efficiency. The company hasn't stopped at what might be termed an applications refresh. It has also automated customer request management: the system determines which office, manager and resource should be alerted for each request and ensures that issues are prioritized correctly and resolved in an appropriate time frame. The payoff? In its most recent earnings call, UTi reported gross revenues up 27 percent and net revenues up 28 percent over the previous year.[17] That represented record levels of quarterly gross and net revenues, operating and net incomes and earnings per share. In the announcement, Roger I. MacFarlane, UTi Worldwide's CEO, noted the market's positive reception to global integrated logistics. He also observed, "The improvement in operating performance in our freight forwarding services . . . reflects the benefits of *increased network density through our global platform* [italics added] as we handled more shipments for new and existing customers."[18] UTi is at the cusp of transforming itself into a major Predictive Business player in the logistics market.

WHERE'S THE PREDICTIVE ELEMENT?

FedEx, UTi and Southwest Airlines are striking examples of real-time businesses. They start from a position that says, "Customers are king and regardless of the conditions that might impact our business operations, we have to serve them as though none of these potentially adverse events impacts them." How will these companies keep their promises as they grow and complexities multiply? The answer lies in the vast stores of data they are now collecting, which can be tapped to discover trends in given scenarios. By applying automated business process and event detection to a raft of historical and current data, they can instantly deploy alternative tactics to overcome the next problem. It is a combination of understanding activities occurring in the *now*, combined with results from past activities, that provides predictive power.

Predictive techniques will help transportation and logistic companies decide which flight plans are most profitable. What the most optimal points are for changing flights crews and drink replenishment. Where they should locate distribution centers and transfer stations. And who their most loyal customers are.

chapter

POWERING RETAIL AND CONSUMER GOODS

RETAIL'S GOLIATH

In the retail world, there is Wal-Mart and there is everybody else. Wal-Mart is an industry giant—the world's largest retailer with annual sales (2004) of over $285 billion. More than 1.6 million people work for Wal-Mart, in over 3,000 stores across the United States plus 1,600 stores overseas. The company boasts that it serves 138 million price-conscious consumers worldwide every week.[1]

Wal-Mart is also a leader in its use of information technology. The company attributes much of its success to heavy investments in IT dating back to the late 1960s.

In 1969, long before competitors, Wal-Mart installed its first computer to track inventory at a distribution center. During the 1970s, Wal-Mart was one of the first retailers to establish a computer terminal network linking stores to distribution centers and the home office. Later, the company added satellite links to enable electronic ordering and invoicing. Over the past several years, this configuration led to the development of Retail Link, a proprietary point-of-sale data network connecting each store to distribution centers and many of Wal-Mart's suppliers.

"One of the misconceptions about Wal-Mart is that we are able to charge low prices because our size gives us the ability to get the best deals from suppliers. Another misconception is that our prices are lower because we offer substandard pay and benefits to our workers," says S. Robson (Rob) Walton, Wal-Mart chairman and son of Wal-Mart founder, Sam Walton. "None of this is true."[2]

"The real key to Wal-Mart's everyday low prices is the company's success at driving unnecessary costs out of the business at every possible link in the supply chain," says Walton.[3] "We pride ourselves on being 'cutting edge' in using technology to get merchandise onto retail shelves," Walton adds.[4] In particular, Retail Link plays a central role in supply chain management.

"A vendor can access our systems, our data, real-time, [to] monitor the sales of their products. They can tell real-time what is selling, what color, how many, what price," David Glass, chairman of the executive committee of the board explained at Wal-Mart's 2005 shareholder meeting.[5] In addition to real-time point-of-sale data, Retail Link includes analytical tools, historical data and six-month sales projections for each product.

"There is no excuse for being out of stock if you are a vendor with Wal-Mart using Retail Link," says Charles Weinacker, co-founder of Pet Friendly, a manufacturer of pet toys that has grown rapidly through sales to Wal-Mart.[6]

"Wal-Mart does not consider itself to be a mere customer of its suppliers," Walton explains. "Our relationships are more like partnerships," in which "Wal-Mart provides suppliers with tools and data to help them better forecast the demand for their products, which, in turn, enables suppliers to more efficiently plan production and delivery schedules."[7]

"Wal-Mart got the jump on then-larger competitors by having the foresight to invest in technology," Walton adds. "Many technologies first adopted by Wal-Mart have become industry standards—because they worked so well for us, and because they proved to be efficiency-enhancing for Wal-Mart, our suppliers, and many other retailers."[8]

RFID: REAL-TIME RETAILING

Wal-Mart is now in the forefront of the introduction of radio frequency identification (RFID) tags in the retail arena. In early 2005, the company began a large-scale trial of the new technology in three distribution centers and 140 stores throughout North Texas and Oklahoma. The company plans to expand the project to include up to 600 stores and 12 additional distribution centers before the end of 2005.[9]

RFID tags are electronic devices that carry information about the item to which they're attached. A tiny antenna is stimulated by an RFID reader to transmit this information. The tags enable retailers to track each item ordered throughout its journey from factory to store shelf.

Target and Albertson's are also experimenting with RFID, while in Europe, Metro Group, Tesco and Marks & Spencer are testing the technology.

RFID will "fundamentally change the way business is done," says Linda Dillman, Wal-Mart chief information officer, by providing visibility into product movement at every step in the supply chain. The benefits "will be shared by supplier, retailer and customer alike."[10]

For the first time, items will be accounted for as quickly as they are placed on or leave retail shelves. No longer will the collection of this data depend upon an army of merchandisers and manufacturer's representatives walking the store floors and manually checking shelves. No matter how many times store shelves are checked, there is an inherent delay in the transmission of information, some of which may not be accurate. The net result is that stock outs are an accepted part of promotions life. At the back end of the supply network, retailers have to build in pre-display slack to ensure they have enough merchandise on the shelves at the start of the promotion. Money is lost and customers get frustrated.

In Wal-Mart stores, the RFID tags will help to ensure that shelves are replenished more quickly, Dillman says. "For example, we found that on a Saturday only one out of four of the out-of-stocks on the shelf actually made it to a picking list [of items that needed to be restocked]."[11] RFID will enable the creation of automatic picking lists and will also help store employees to locate merchandise in a store's stockroom, she explained. Wal-Mart is testing RFID readers that help workers find the products for restocking by beeping more frequently as they get closer to the needed case.

Readers positioned at the stores' receiving bay doors, exits to the sales floor and near box crushers will also provide information about the dwell times of merchandise—the length of time that an item is in the store.

All of the data collected from RFID tags is fed into Wal-Mart's Retail Link network for the benefit of suppliers.

"RFID can provide more accurate accountability in the supply chain, better management of in-store inventory and better demand planning," says Weinacker of Pet Friendly. "One specific benefit of RFID technology is that we can know a retailer is short on our product inventory, sometimes before they do. This allows us to manufacture and ship additional inventory 'ahead of demand.' The biggest benefit to Pet Friendly is that with RFID tags on our products, we can capture and record every stage and event in the product's movement through our supply chains."[12]

Once RFID-driven "Wal-Mart speed" is widely established, the dynamics of retail will change radically. Instead of suppliers pushing product to the customer, consumer pulls from store shelves will trigger inventory replenishment. This is what AMR Research calls the Demand Driven Supply Network.[13] Efficient retailer response to consumer demand depends on just-in-time inventory synchronized with suppliers' production schedules, transportation schedules, and warehouse fulfillment demands. Real-time, pull-driven inventory management holds the promise of giving customers what they want, wherever and whenever they want it while ensuring that inventories are kept at optimal levels.

NEW CHANNELS TO MARKET

Discount warehouses such as Costco and out-of-town discount malls have become prime shopping destinations in the United States. Meanwhile, some of the fastest growing retailers are focused on niche markets. Steve & Barry's University Sportswear, for example, has doubled sales for each of the past two years to become what Forbes magazine called "the fastest-growing retailer you never heard of."[14]

In contrast, one of the most prominent examples of retail diversification is Amazon. The online retailer has moved far beyond its role as a bookseller to become an online shopping emporium, offering everything from electronics to fashions and housewares while maintaining a unified customer experience. As Jeff Bezos, Amazon chief executive, explains, "We use the term customer experience broadly. It includes every customer-facing aspect of our business. . . . The customer experience we create is by far the most important driver of our business."[15]

Hence, the biggest change impacting the retail industry over the past decade has been the emergence of online shopping. Electronic outlets have eclipsed brick-and-mortar stores in terms of sales growth. Online consumer retail spending grew by 26 percent to a record level of $117 billion in 2004, according to comScore Networks, a market research firm that specializes in this field.[16]

In the early days of e-commerce, online stores were seen as a big threat to the traditional retailer, but the latest market data suggests that retail industry leaders may in fact be the big winners on the Internet. Six of the top 15 performers during the 2004 holiday season were the online storefronts of traditional department stores. "While it's clear that a broad range of online merchants saw a strong season, multi-channel retailers were standouts," said Dan Hess, com Score senior vice president. "Many of the nation's leading retail brands flexed their muscle this season, with strategies including faster delivery options, significant site redesigns and effective cross-channel promotions." Among the top online retailers cited in the study were Home Depot, Neiman Marcus and Wal-Mart.[17]

These and many other retailers now see the Internet as an important distribution channel and differentiate themselves in the online marketplace through their service offerings. Tesco.com, the top UK retailer, for example, offers home delivery and makes "customers who bought this also purchased that" suggestions in the manner pioneered by Amazon.com. In its attempt to keep customers "sticky," Tesco also remembers user preferences and cross-sells discounts on car insurance, for example, to shoppers who buy groceries at its Web site.

MULTIPLE TOUCH POINTS

Consumers expect the Nordstrom experience, or the Safeway experience or indeed the Wal-Mart experience, whether they are shopping at a local store or on one of these retailers' Web sites. Yet many IT architectures fail to capture, much less integrate, all of a retailer's customer touch points. Elements such as merchandising, store layout, payment options and return policies must carry across all of a company's operations and, to be truly effective, they must be conducted in real time. The consumer, for example, should be able to purchase an item online and return it to a store. Similarly, when a customer is unable to find exactly the product he or she needs in a store, the clerk should be able to refer the customer to the retailer's Web site if the item is available there.

Each customer interaction has to be tracked so the retailer can create or enhance a fine-grained knowledge base about individual customers and their preferences. This knowledge is critical to predicting the what, when and where of the next sale.

Retail has plenty of ways to engage with customers but they are often after the fact—after a sale, in most cases. When customers buy something, the retailer may send them a discount voucher for their next purchase but isn't that too late? Will the offer be relevant to the customer's needs next time around or will it represent

The Amazon.com Phenomenon

Amazon.com CEO Jeff Bezos has a singular focus on customers: his goal is to build earth's most customer-centric company. "We start with the customer and work backwards," he explains.[1] This has been Amazon's mantra since the company was founded 10 years ago, and Bezos consistently emphasizes the point.

"At Amazon.com, we use the term customer experience broadly. It includes every customer-facing aspect of our business—from our product prices to our selection, from our website's user interface to how we package and ship items. The customer experience we create is by far the most important driver of our business," Bezos wrote in his 2003 letter to shareholders.[2]

The three pillars of customer experience are selection, price and convenience, he adds. In terms of providing a broad selection of goods, Bezos' uncompromising goal is to "build a place where people can come to find and discover anything they may want to buy online." [3] He believes there are "years and years of work ahead" to build out the product selection, despite the fact that Amazon is adding numerous new categories to its U.S. and international Web sites at a rapid pace—for example, loose diamonds on the U.S. Web site and magazines on the Japanese site.[4]

Customer convenience is the bedrock of the Amazon experience, but Bezos is always looking for ways to improve, whether it's adding more book reviews or launching Amazon Prime, a flat fee subscription for express shipping. Amazon Prime is "changing the way they [customers] use and think about Amazon.com," says Bezos.[5] Customers are more likely to turn to the Web site for last minute purchases than in the past, he explains.

Amazon's pricing strategy does not attempt to maximize margin percentages, but instead seeks to drive maximum value for customers, Bezos states. The average customer discount on books and DVDs, for example, increased by 3 percent in the first quarter of 2005 versus the same period a year earlier.[6]

"Wall Street gets in a kerfuffle when we lower product prices and invest heavily in the future. So we tell them—don't buy our stock—instead buy our products and enjoy our investments. If we take care of customers, the stock will take care of itself in the long term," he says boldly.[7]

Indeed, investors took a dim view of Amazon's slowing revenue growth and heavy spending on improved infrastructure and IT during 2004 and early 2005, but all was forgiven when the company reported higher than expected second quarter results in July 2005.[8] Amazon's shares jumped on the news and hopes that Bezos' ambitious strategies could pay off.

a generic marketing effort hoping to find an interested shopper? Will it be personalized to the type of items this consumer typically purchases? What is needed are real-time relationship-building tools that can, for example, give repeat or big-ticket customers discounts on their next basket of purchases—whether they are shopping online or in person.

PROACTIVELY MANAGING CUSTOMERS

As mentioned earlier in the chapter, in an RFID-enabled retail world, the entire customer interaction changes. Instead of responding to perceived demand at the area level, retailers now have the chance to get close to customers at the individual store level. This is achieved by applying pattern recognition techniques to in-store sales over a given time interval. At its most extreme, this means the retailer might identify a one-time buy and later a repeat purchase by the same customer. Assembling information about how customers behave also allows the retailer to tailor promotional activities. Predictability is achieved because the retailer is responding to consumer-specific events that display given patterns *at the time those events occur*. In turn, the retailer can apply the pull stocking principles described earlier so that shelves are not only adequately stocked but are continuously replenished to reflect changes in demand.

From the manufacturers' perspectives, there is much more information on which to take appropriate actions. I anticipate that, in time, companies will have answers to such essential questions as "what goods are in transit?", "what's coming into my warehouse?" and "what's coming from my suppliers?" Armed with this information, suppliers and distributors will be able to dynamically reroute in-transit goods.

THE BIG/SMALL RETAIL PARADOX

There is a retail paradox that large companies are always striving to overcome. The small retailer develops customer intimacy as a survival mechanism. In the single store outlet, staff members know their customers by sight and name after serving them for years. They don't usually need much computing power to know individual customer buying preferences. Intimacy goes one step further because, in this scenario, individual staff members "own" individual customers. It is this direct, continuing human interaction that makes certain upscale retailers highly profitable. In turn, these stores have a pretty good idea of what kinds of products their customers will buy and they stock accordingly.

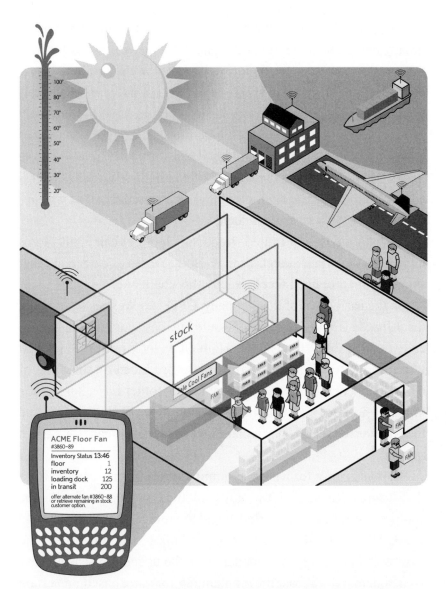

How to Orchestrate Logistics When the Temperature Changes Quickly and You Need to Maximize Market Opportunity and Customer Satisfaction. While some companies might wait too long for significant buying signals, Predictive Businesses proactively identify the seemingly unrelated events (weather condition, inventory levels, buying trends) to coordinate and re-allocate assets faster to take advantage of the constantly changing market.

Large retail organizations cannot achieve the same level of intimacy using the same methods. There are many reasons for this, but margin pressure, for instance, does not allow retailers to expend the same amount of employee dollars per dollar of revenue as their small competitors. Also, large retailers have the constant headache of juggling complex inventories among thousands of stores across multiple geographies. Therefore, large retailers have to rely on technology as the *basis* for fostering lasting relationships and for delivering the right combination of products that will appeal to the largest consumer segments.

Specialty retailer Limited Brands, with more than 3,800 stores including Victoria's Secret, Bath & Body Works and several other shopping mall brands, faced exactly this challenge.

In the early days of the company, CEO Les Wexner figured out that Limited Brands' customers would buy based upon what was locally fashionable. He visited certain cities looking for trends that were unique to the area and then mass-produced on the basis of what he discovered. Wexner knew his customer base, sensed the kinds of product his customers were likely to find attractive and then delivered just as a particular trend went mainstream for a given market.

Wexner's nose for what was coming next was the secret to Limited Brands' success. But it only took the company so far. As the company grew and diversified, it had to predict seasonal styles and trends 18 months ahead of time, place bulk production orders and ensure that products were available for the upcoming season. Creating a demand forecast meant planning forward, based on certain broad demand assumptions. At a global level, this sounds reasonable, but at the local level it is dangerous; there are always regional variations in taste and spending power. Demand forecasts can lead to situations where product is available in one location but out of stock elsewhere.

Gallo—In Right Time

When E & J Gallo Winery employees, customers, distributors, and suppliers need up-to-date information, they need look no further than the Grapevine Portal, an internal view and four-way, external view of company information and procedures.

"Our approach was to leverage a single portal infrastructure to provide appropriate information to all elements of our supply chain—from grape growers to distributors, to retail stores, to restaurants," says Kent Kushar, E & J Gallo's chief information officer.[1]

The Gallo portal is updated as needed—by the hour or by the minute—depending on the urgency and context of the information. Daily sales data, for example, are updated every morning. Sales managers can also launch queries to obtain additional information and analysis on a 24/7 basis. "There are incredible amounts of analysis done on that information. Production planning uses it. Strategic planning uses it. The consensus forecast people use it and the demand planning people use it."

In Gallo's glass factory, where wine bottles are made, managers and production workers view real-time data on flat screen TVs throughout the plant. These production dashboards provide up-to-the-moment, actionable performance metrics. Gallo can then leverage the information to make immediate decisions. "There are some aspects of our business that operate on real-time systems, such as the production facilities, but generally we look at 'right-time data,'" Kushar explained in a recent conversation. This means delivering the right data to the right people at the time it is needed.

How does Kushar see a role for predictive technology in wine production, packaging, distribution and marketing?

Predictive is going to allow us to take a look at cross-functional issues. If something happens in one function, what is the real effect on other functions? What happens, for example, if you run out of labels on a bottling line? What happens is the machine is going to stop. So what is the impact on the cellar when that happens? Well, the tank that is feeding the line holds 10,000 gallons. That tank is scheduled to accept another wine at a certain time. That other wine is being staged right now. It may be on a truck coming from one of our wineries. If we have to stop the line for 5 or 30 minutes, what is that going to mean? The truck drivers need two hours' notice to change their schedule. So we need to know at least three hours in advance that we are going to run out of labels, if we are to do something to fix the problem.

Packaging Tribal Wisdom

One of the most important roles that Kushar sees for predictive technology is capturing the accumulated knowledge of Gallo's outstanding, long-term employees.

"We have some very interesting [bottling] lines. Some are new, some are old. We have one [line] in particular for international orders and it wasn't running properly, and it had not been running well for a week. George, a 30-year veteran in Gallo's bottling room, came over and walked around that machine . . . just walked around it for an hour . . . and listened. He came back and said: 'Do this, this, this, and this.' And that line was whistling along two hours later."

As Kushar notes, "Many really smart people tried to fix it for a week and they couldn't. But one guy with the right historical context fixed it in two hours." George retired two years ago. So now one of Kushar's goals is to package that "tribal wisdom."

Beyond preventive maintenance, it is a matter of recording scenarios, detecting and correlating production events, devising instructions on how to prevent breakdown, and taking a strong look at what's happening right now. "We're working on this [challenge] as fast as we can. It's not to replace people. It is actually to give people the opportunity to make fixes that would otherwise cause undue delays."

Can predictive technology do what Wexler sensed intuitively? The answer, at least in theory, is yes. Predictive technology, like Wexler, relies upon patterns and trends that are observed over decades. Hemlines rise and fall. Perfumes go in and out of favor. But to the experienced merchandiser (and the automated rules engine) these are not random events. They follow predictable patterns that can be identified when historical and real-time data are correlated.

PREDICTIVE BUSINESS IN HEALTHCARE AND LIFE SCIENCE

TECHNOLOGY HAS MADE enormous contributions to medicine over recent years with the emergence of computerized scanners, miniature heart defibrillators, surgical robots and many other breakthrough inventions. Yet when it comes to record keeping and processes, the healthcare sector has hardly changed in decades. Visit your primary care physician, and the chances are high that she or he will make handwritten notes and then perhaps dictate them into a tape recorder for somebody else to transcribe. If you switch to a new doctor, your medical history may not follow you. Many hospitals are similarly lagging when it comes to the use of basic technology tools for storing medical records. Indeed, most U.S. medical institutions have much more electronic information on a patient's financial and insurance history than on the patient's medical record.

The healthcare industry has taken a tepid approach to adopting information technology. The typical U.S. hospital invests 2 to 3 percent of revenue in IT, compared to 12 to 15 percent of the top line in many other industries.[1] Only 3 percent of U.S. hospitals have computerized order entry and patient records.[2] This underinvestment in IT has contributed to spiraling healthcare costs that have drawn the attention of President George W. Bush and the U.S. Congress. "Despite spending over $1.6 trillion on health care as a Nation, there are still serious concerns about high costs, avoidable medical errors, administrative inefficiencies, and poor coordination—all of which are closely connected to the failure to incorporate health information technology into our health care system," the President's press secretary said in a January 2005 briefing.[3]

However, big changes are afoot. National health IT coordinator Dr. David Brailer has called for most Americans to have electronic health records within 10 years.[4] This initiative is aimed at creating personal health records that patients, doctors, hospitals and other healthcare providers can securely access via the Internet no matter where a patient seeks medical care.

"The use of electronic health records and other information technology will transform our health care system by reducing medical errors, minimizing paperwork hassles, lowering costs and improving quality of care," Mike Leavitt, Health and Human Services Secretary, said in announcing the first steps toward creating this system: establishing standards to achieve interoperability. "Federal agencies—who pay for more than one-third of all health care in the country—[will] work with private-sector health care providers and employers in developing and adopting an architecture, standards and certification process," Secretary Leavitt noted.[5]

The European Union is moving in the same direction, with an e-health initiative to digitize patient data and put it online by the end of this year. Moreover, the UK government has undertaken a large-scale effort aimed at updating the information infrastructure of the National Health Service. By October 2004 it had awarded private sector contracts worth a total of £6.2 billion[6] to create electronic health records for 50 million people as well as shared, centralized back office services for medical facilities. The NHS National Programme for Information Technology will allow doctors to access patient records, create prescriptions and book hospital appointments—all electronically.[7]

Spending on healthcare information technology (HIT) is now growing rapidly, according to consultant Sheldon I. Dorenfest and Associates, with U.S. spending projected to rise from $25.8 billion in 2004 to $30.5 billion in 2006.[8]

WHY NOW?

As the healthcare sector moves into the digital age, it is instructive to examine why it has taken so long to apply basic digital record keeping processes to the practice of medicine. Part of the answer seems to lie in an apparent reluctance on the part of doctors to take the time to adapt to the use of IT. The bigger issue that has dogged the U.S. health sector, in particular, is concern about privacy and confidentiality. Electronic records containing sensitive information are difficult to protect, as we have seen in the financial services sector, and consumers are wary that their medical information may fall into the wrong hands. Moreover, in a system that relies heavily upon healthcare insurance, some fear that negative information on electronic health records available to all doctors may prevent individuals from obtaining insurance in the future.

This is a valid and widespread concern, but it is based on a misunderstanding. In reality, U.S. medical insurance companies already have electronic health records on approximately 15 million Americans and Canadians. This information is compiled by the Medical Information Bureau (MIB) in a central database shared by insurance companies. About 600 insurance firms use the services of the MIB, primarily to obtain information about individual life and health insurance applicants. Individuals who apply for life or health insurance are typically asked to provide health information and/or be examined by a doctor. The insurance company may then report this information to the MIB, where it is fed into the database in the form of codes that represent certain medical conditions such as diabetes or high blood pressure. MIB records are not subject to the same privacy laws as medical health records.[9]

If it is possible for the insurance industry to create a centralized database, why has the healthcare industry been unable to do so? The answer is multifaceted.

On the regulatory front, healthcare providers must adhere to strict privacy laws that preclude sharing of information without the explicit permission of the patient. They also face the burden of protecting the privacy of electronic records.

Another big inhibitor to the adoption of electronic health records has been complexity. Medical records typically include images and data in multiple formats. This is in sharp contrast to the structured data found in financial records.

Although the insurance industry has a strong financial incentive to create a digital repository of individuals' medical information, healthcare providers have seen little incentive to collaborate with one another on record keeping. Because they are paid according to the volume of services they provide, doctors and hospitals have tended to maximize those services, even if it means repeating tests, for example, rather than finding the results of the same tests performed elsewhere.

In a move to address this issue, Medicare has set up a trial at 277 hospitals in which it's paying higher fees for higher quality results in five treatment areas. "We're trying to create the busi-

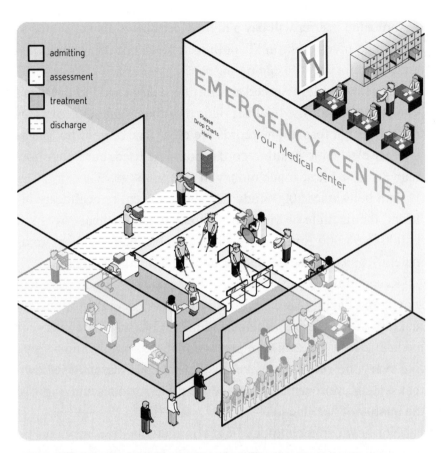

The Bottleneck at the Emergency Center (EC). Emergency centers constantly deal with fluctuating volumes and prioritization. For many hospitals, the EC is the main conduit to hospital admissions. Synchronized coordination is essential as resource decisions are made minute-to-minute to ensure the highest quality care while maintaining financial prosperity.

ness case for more coordinated, efficient care, and inevitably that means more investment in tech," says Dr. Mark McClellan, Medicare administrator.[10] Private insurers are following suit by offering hospitals incentives based on performance. If a hospital achieves an above-average rate of success in a particular practice area, for example, the insurer will pay a higher fee. This is also expected to encourage investment in IT, both as a means of improving outcomes and for record keeping purposes.

It is now widely agreed within the healthcare industry and among payers for medical services that the advantages of electronic health information records are clear. The issue is no longer whether electronic health records should be used, but rather how many lives and how much money they might save.

In a bellwether 2000 study that shook the entire healthcare industry, the Institute of Medicine estimated that medical errors kill 45,000 to 98,000 Americans each year in hospitals, with approximately 7,000 of these deaths attributable to medication errors.[11]

Responding to these findings, the Agency for Healthcare Research and Quality said healthcare providers needed to focus on making systems improvements and not on blaming caregivers for medical errors. "Health care professionals are simply human and, like everyone else, they make mistakes. But research has shown that system improvements can reduce the error rates and improve the quality of health care."[12]

Not only can technology help eliminate medical mistakes by making health information more accessible to patients and providers, it can also reduce costs as much as 10 percent by saving time, reducing duplication and waste and improving efficiency, according to the Department of Health and Human Services.[13]

VETERANS ADMINISTRATION

The Veterans Administration, which runs 158 hospitals and over 850 outpatient clinics as well as numerous nursing homes and other facilities in the United States, was an early adopter of electronic health records. The VA, in fact, has had automated infor-

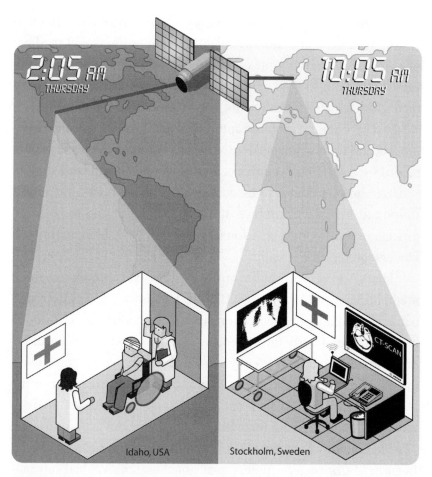

How Long Before the Extent of Your Injury is Known. The event of a midnight car accident dictates critical response, and the patient may not survive to see the head trauma specialist who will be back in 6 hours. The eager network of care providers enables service beyond borders and the rapid identification of expertise that can be accessed when it is needed.

mation systems in its medical facilities since 1985. The current VA system for medical records is called VistA, for Veterans Integrated Systems Technology Architecture.

VistA brings together all the relevant computerized information pertaining to a patient and makes it available to all VA medical staff. With over 100 separate modules, VistA can be configured to fit any type of healthcare organization, from clinics and medical practices to nursing homes and large hospitals. Doctors can tap into the system to find a complete history of the patient's treatments, doctor visits, test results, medications and much more.

VistA's imaging system captures clinical images, scanned documents and non-text data files to create a singular electronic health record for a patient, instantly accessible at any clinical workstation. "VistA allows a doctor to essentially treat the patient holistically, to look at the bigger picture, to diagnose better and to be more precise in treatment," says Jonathan Perlin, MD, PhD, acting VA Undersecretary for Health.[14]

The VA is also in the forefront of auto ID bar-code–enabled medication administration (ABMA). The automated system dispenses each patient's medications into a bar-coded bin. Bar-coded bracelets also identify the patient and the nurses who administer his or her medications. The VA's system has been shown to radically reduce medication errors. Robert Krawisz, executive director of the National Patient Safety Foundation, has said that the benefits of automating medication administration using bar codes are significant: "The technology's impact at VA hospitals so far has been amazing." In an *FDA Consumer* article, it was noted that the VA had substantially reduced medication errors by using bar codes as part of its medication administration processes in VA hospitals. "For example, the VA Medical Center in Topeka, Kansas has reported that bar coding reduced its medication error rate by 86 percent over a nine-year period."[15]

Another VA initiative set to begin in early 2006 is Medicare e-prescribing, or the electronic communication of prescriptions among doctors, patients and pharmacists. By backing this initiative, the federal government aims to encourage its growth. E-prescribing can improve patient safety and reduce avoidable healthcare costs, by decreasing prescription errors due to hard-to-read physician handwriting and by automating the process of checking for drug interactions and allergies. E-prescribing can also help make sure that patients and health professionals have the best and latest medical information at hand when they make important decisions about choosing medicines, enabling beneficiaries to get the most benefits at the lowest cost.[16]

For all of their advantages, electronic medical records, systems that enable doctors to enter orders electronically and systems that track medications are not cure-alls. Mark Leavitt, medical director of Healthcare Information and Management Systems Society, suggests these systems should include decision support mechanisms such as alerts, reminders and dose suggestions to further reduce medical errors.[17]

JUST THE BEGINNING

Electronic health records are just the first step toward what some consider the digital hospital of the future. When records including treatment and outcome details are stored, they provide a historical base for decision support and even predictive systems. The data can be analyzed to judge alternative treatments (such as heart bypass surgery versus angioplasty) by looking at how quickly patients are discharged and whether they're readmitted. The data can also be used to study which medicines work best, to identify patients at risk and to review the performance of individual physicians.

In other words, the Predictive Business principles of observation, pattern matching and probability can be applied to determining how best to treat hospital patients. The healthcare system has extensive and complete data about patient history, although at present it is often locked up in multiple systems or paper files.

Once that information is released and real-time data is added, predictive techniques can be applied.

Medstar Health, which runs seven hospitals in the Baltimore/ Washington, DC, area, has created an Emergency Insight System, accessing medical records from a data warehouse and combining them with live information gathered from other departments. According to Dr. Craig Feied, one of the system's designers, it improves care in several ways. "Because the system marries past and present data, clinicians make decisions in the context of complete information."[18] The system allows dynamic queries for more detailed patient information, and local data analysis is just a mouse click away. MedStar is planning a wireless network that will allow doctors to access the system from handheld computers and other mobile devices.

Combining historical data with real-time data, Washington Hospital Center, one of MedStar's facilities in Washington, DC, identifies the risks associated with clinical procedures and treatments using reporting and analysis software. The hospital plans to use the results to identify patients for whom certain treatments or drugs may be risky (based on clinical patterns and demographics such as age) and deliver that information to physicians.[19]

When Brigham and Women's Hospital in Massachusetts began computerizing its system for physician orders in 1993, it was one of the first hospitals in the country to do so. In 2000, the hospital extended the Computerized Physician Order Entry (CPOE) system to outpatient clinics and centers. The hospital has also developed a system for pharmacists that facilitates real-time review of patients' records and test results to detect adverse drug reactions. This year, Brigham and Women's will implement electronic medication administration records and patient bar coding to further reduce the possibility of medication errors.[20]

As these examples show, real-time information can make a real difference for hospital patients. Children's Hospital of Pittsburgh, Pennsylvania, has also been recognized for its use of advanced HIT systems. In pediatrics, the problems of medication errors have been particularly acute but Children's has practically eliminated errors that cause serious harm. As Laura Landro reported in the *Wall Street Journal*, "Now doctors can enter their orders from any computer in the hospital; the system automatically calculates appropriate drug doses based on a child's age and weight. It also flags possible allergies or drug interactions, and zaps the finished order to the pharmacy." Errors in transcribing doctor notes have been eliminated entirely.[21] The rate of medication errors that cause harm has dropped from .04 per thousand doses to .01 per thousand.[22]

The value of healthcare information systems reaches beyond cost savings and minimizing errors. "Healthcare is about to undergo a major transformation enabled by IT," says Tom Miller, president of the IT division, Siemens Medical Solutions. "It will emerge in the ability to capture and analyze all points of information to develop best practices and, ultimately, add to the body of clinical knowledge." The benefits will include better prevention, earlier diagnosis, targeted therapies and improved clinical outcomes for individual patients, he predicts.[23]

Siemens' approach to hospital information systems is based on a work flow model rather than a transaction model. Its hospital IT systems manage transactions and data as well as the process of healthcare delivery and interactions among healthcare providers. The result is streamlined operations and work flow. In addition, critical symptoms and diseases can be detected sooner and treated more effectively.[24]

Another innovation recently announced by the German company is a bedside monitor that provides patients with entertainment

(TV, videos, Internet, etc.). When controlled by a nurse or doctor, this same monitor transforms into a point-of-care device, providing access to essential patient data.[25]

HEALTHCARE CLINIC 2015

Turn the clock forward 10 years and where will we be? If President Bush's initiative is successful, most Americans will have electronic health records. If the recent trend toward pay for performance is any indication, healthcare providers will be far more inclined to adopt technologies that improve efficiencies and—we hope—the quality of medical care. Perhaps it is too much to hope for a real decline in the cost of healthcare but an end to the spiraling increase might be achievable.

We can also look forward to a significant reduction in medical mistakes and, let us hope, a patient-centric approach to the practice of medicine, akin to the best practices of customer-centric companies in other industries.

Self-service medicine that empowers individuals to manage their own health services, in much the same way that diabetics check their glucose levels, also appears feasible. Instead of visiting a doctor's office for a strep test, the patient will buy the test over-the-counter and relay the results to the doctor electronically.

Trusted online information resources will help consumers find answers to their medical questions. Telemedicine surely has to expand to permit doctors and patients to communicate more efficiently on the phone or via e-mail, to save time and reduce costs.

Doctors' offices and other care facilities will be linked via secure networks, to facilitate communications among doctors and between doctors and patients. A system of this sort is already in place in Tacoma, Washington, where 200 medical offices and care facilities are linked to a Siemens Soarian community access system. "Through this initiative, the entire physician office staff benefits from an interactive, secure workflow where they can send each other secure messages, respond to or forward received messages, and view patient demographics and clinical information," says Dr. Donald Rucker, chief medical officer of Siemens Medical Solutions.[26] Through The Network, patients can request prescription refills and referrals, make appointments, get billing information and communicate with their physicians. They can update their individual electronic health records. The system gives physicians a means to correspond with their patients securely while being reimbursed for their time and expertise.[27]

The big breakthroughs will come when predictive techniques are applied widely to medicine, so that looming problems can be addressed. We may wear monitoring devices that feed real-time data to our doctors. Perhaps doctors will be alerted if a patient has missed a checkup. Patients might receive reminders that they need to schedule appointments.

In the future, we will relate to our healthcare providers in much the same way that we do to banks and credit card companies today. We will expect our doctors to have up-to-the-minute information about every aspect of our health. We will also expect to receive electronic alerts—via e-mail or text messages on our phones—if a test result shows something unexpected or worrisome. Virtual visits with our doctors will be the norm.

We certainly will not expect to spend time in the waiting room on the rare occasions when we need to meet our doctors in person. Work flow systems will ensure that waiting times are minimized. On-site pharmacies will dispense medications.

Cerner, a healthcare software developer, has plans to open a clinic of the future at its Kansas City headquarters. The proof-of-concept facility will demonstrate how efficiently a physician's practice can operate while providing care to Cerner employees and others. "We believe that the physician office of the future will be one without waiting rooms, with exam rooms that were built with the patient's needs in mind, and with technology prevalent throughout. Everything, including the payment process, has been redesigned to deliver what healthcare consumers take for granted in other industries," said Jeff Townsend, Cerner chief of staff.[28]

KEEPING THE EQUIPMENT GOING

Hospitals and clinics are already packed with sophisticated instruments and equipment and will no doubt be even more so in the future. Maintaining that equipment is critical to patient care and represents a growing challenge.

Philips Medical Systems, a leading supplier of medical equipment, has addressed this issue with a recently upgraded, remote, real-time monitoring network. One of the largest networks of its kind worldwide, it links to Philips equipment (including X-ray, ultrasound, MRI tomography, radiation oncology and patient monitoring systems) in 1,300 global hospitals. The network enables Philips technicians to access its medical equipment remotely, without disabling the machines, to perform system diagnostics, identify and solve problems as well as conduct proactive maintenance.[29] This is clearly the way of the future as the healthcare sector becomes increasingly dependent on sophisticated technology.

It is not difficult to imagine similar service networks supporting critical HIT systems in the future. Proactive systems maintenance and problem solving, as well as software upgrades and other updates, might all be performed remotely via secure networks.

Although it may seem far-fetched, similar principles can also be applied to patient care. Recently, devices have been put into the hands of patients that relay information back to their physicians. A study by Accenture indicates that patients are prepared to adopt diagnostic technology if it adds to their quality of life and provides a demonstrable comfort factor in their care programs: "The vast majority, roughly 69 percent, report wanting to see their test results and being comfortable as the only ones who do. Most want to know if and when their results are outside the expected range and would be comfortable having their doctor call to discuss the findings."[30] The authors are quick to acknowledge the many hurdles facing new technology. At the top of the list are questions about who pays and how long it will take government administrators to approve such devices. However, the fact that there is such an overwhelmingly positive response implies that home-based care is something the public—especially the over-65 age group—is prepared to embrace with enthusiasm.

GOING WIRELESS

Wireless laptops and PDAs are rapidly becoming medical tools. Mobility, flexibility and speed make them providers' favored devices to access medical records. Whenever and wherever patient information is needed, in the surgical suite or in an outpatient clinic, wireless devices come into play.

In an October 2004 study of wireless adoption in various industries, market research firm IDC found that more than 80 percent of the 34 healthcare organizations polled said that they have deployed wireless networks or plan to deploy them in the next 12 months.[31] And according to the 2005 Healthcare Information and Management Systems Society Leadership Survey published in February 2005, 79 percent of healthcare executives said they would use wireless information systems by the end of the year, while 54 percent said they would use handheld devices.[32]

Doctors were early adopters of PDAs, even before these had wireless capabilities. Electronic versions of medical reference texts were among the most popular PDA applications, at first. Today, the devices are used to access medical records as well as for communications, replacing the ubiquitous pager.

RFID—A PANACEA?

RFID tracking devices open up a range of new possibilities for healthcare. For instance, patients could be assigned tags as they enter a medical facility. As they pass through the assessment and treatment processes, they could be electronically tracked. The benefits are significant.

Caregivers will always know where patients can be located. In crowded emergency rooms, this would be a boon to managing patient flow and safety. Staff would simply enter the name of the patient on a computer to determine his or her location. From a treatment perspective, clinical staff would no longer have to visually inspect a wristband to ensure they're dealing with the right person.

Smart tags might also be applied to medical instruments. This could reduce the potential for using unfit equipment and, when merged with patient RFID tag information, could form the basis for ensuring staff have the correct tools for the job at hand. In busy departments where instruments are loaded onto portable carts, locating required equipment would be much easier. Currently, RFIDs are primarily employed in tracking hospital supplies. This makes sense because hospitals typically lose 8 to 12 percent of their billable items.[33]

In a leading-edge medical application of RFID tagging, ProPath, a Dallas-based pathology laboratory, recently began using the technology to track biopsy specimens and Pap smears sent to its facilities. The company says that the RFID system will accelerate sample processing and improve record keeping while dramatically reducing human error. ProPath processes 1,500 to 2,000 samples daily. Any complication that arises in processing a sample can hinder diagnosis and treatment, not to mention the costs in terms of time and resources for reprocessing.

RFID tags are affixed to specimens upon arrival at the lab. The tags provide real-time status throughout processing, and, because they track when and by whom specimens have been handled, process control, technician accountability and productivity are measurably improved.

"The systems enable us to fully automate several of the most manual, and thereby problem-prone, laboratory processes, allowing our staff to focus on activities that enhance sample quality and accelerate processing times," said Krista Crews, ProPath executive director. "As a result, we are expecting a 15–20 percent reduction in overall processing times, allowing us to deliver results faster and more securely, to more efficiently use existing resources and, most importantly, to ensure patients' safety and privacy."[34]

In the hospital setting, similar systems could be used to tag drugs and radioisotopes, providing the ability to trace inventory from source through to use. However, progress in the hospital use of RFID technology has been slow. Although the FDA has yet to mandate RFID adoption, it has recommended the tagging of unit-level drugs that are likely to be counterfeited. This is to be completed by 2006. The FDA has also called for the tagging of all drugs at the pallet, case and unit levels by 2007.[35] Datamonitor observes, "The existing FDA mandate on hospital drug bar coding and the abandoned JHACO proposals to use bar coding for achieving patient safety goals can be interpreted as a step back for RFID adoption for healthcare in the near future as the mandates do not stipulate the use of this more advanced technology."[36] The same report notes, "Out-of-date medicine is currently a huge issue for improving patient safety. Medicine expiration dates often go under the radar, and at times when they are being dealt with, it has to be done manually, with the nurse checking each label—a very time-consuming task."

There is certainly no shortage of technology tools for healthcare, and there is now widespread recognition that IT has much to offer in the medical field—both in terms of gathering information and in analyzing it to create predictive tools that will enable doctors to enhance the quality of healthcare services. Yet to be determined, however, is whether all hospitals, not only large health groups and prestigious teaching hospitals, will be able to find the capital to invest in this technology. It seems inevitable that there will be "haves" and "have nots" in the healthcare sector, and there will be industry consolidation as hospitals join forces to address the issue. In other industries, natural attrition sorts out those companies that make best use of IT from those that fail to keep pace. In healthcare, local access to doctors and hospitals is, however, essential, and it may be that medical "payers" will need to participate in ensuring that the availability of electronic health records become widely available and securely managed. Only then will the full value of IT in healthcare begin to be achieved using predictive techniques.

chapter

ENERGY EFFICIENCY

POWER SWITCHES

The energy industry has been buffeted by world events, politics, and economic change over the past decade. War in the Middle East, terrorism threats, hurricanes in the Gulf of Mexico and the economic expansion of China have all contributed to a recent, sharp increase in the price of oil.

Meanwhile, safety and environmental concerns—in the wake of the Chernobyl disaster and other nuclear accidents—have prevented the construction of nuclear plants in the United States and several other countries. Renewable energy resources have failed to live up to their promise, to date, and deregulation of energy utilities has been stalled in most parts of the United States (and resisted in parts of Europe) following the Enron energy trading scandal.

As this is written, U.S. energy policy is once again hitting the headlines. The U.S. Senate has passed an energy bill long sought by

President George W. Bush. However, this bill differs in several respects from the House version, signaling a protracted political battle.[1]

The issues that will be hotly debated range from proposals for drilling in Alaska's Arctic National Wildlife Refuge to a controversial liability waiver for a gasoline additive that pollutes drinking water. Yet with the price of crude oil topping $60 a barrel in July of 2005, the pressure on Congress to enact an energy bill is high. News reports suggest that the legislation most likely to emerge could open the door to a new generation of U.S. nuclear power plants, a new natural-gas pipeline from Alaska to the mainland United States and billions of dollars in subsidies for energy producers.[2]

The outcome of this debate is, of course, still uncertain. Indeed, dealing with political, regulatory and economic uncertainties has been the only constant in the energy utilities industry for many years.

These are not the sort of uncertainties that predictive technology can address. We can, however, narrow some of the other risks and challenges that energy companies face.

ALWAYS ON

Modern life revolves around the constant availability of electricity. When power outages occur, daily life is turned upside down and business processes grind to a halt. Never was this made more apparent than on August 14, 2003, when the northeastern United States and southern Canada suffered the worst power blackout in history. Areas affected included eight U.S. states and a Canadian province, Ontario. Approximately 50 million customers were impacted for up to 13 hours.

Much effort has gone into investigating why this huge blackout occurred and how such failures may be avoided in the future. Not surprisingly, real-time information and predictive techniques have an important role to play in keeping the lights on.

To understand what when wrong and how it might have been avoided, it is instructive to review key events that led to the cascading blackout as described in the Interim Report of the U.S.–Canada Power System Outage Task Force.[3]

- The blackout was triggered by three high-voltage transmission lines that short-circuited when they came into contact with trees. These lines were operated by FirstEnergy (FE), a diversified energy business with seven electricity operating companies serving 4.4 million customers in Ohio, Pennsylvania, and New Jersey.

- FE's control room alarm system failed, so operators did not know about the problem.

- The loss of the three lines resulted in too much electricity flowing onto other nearby lines, which caused them to overload.

- Simultaneously, there was a problem at the Midwest Independent System Operator (MISO), the entity coordinating power transmission in the region.

- MISO's system analysis tools weren't performing effectively on the date of the blackout, according to the task force report, so MISO was unaware of FirstEnergy's growing problem.

- The report found that MISO's reliability coordinators were using outdated data to support real-time monitoring.

The task force's follow-up report a year after the blackout pointed to the lack of real-time information as a significant contributor to the massive outage. It also identified "a clear need for improved real-time tools that would enable operators across a broad regional area to view a common screen and discuss an evolving problem at an early stage in its development."[4]

Perhaps it is in the nature of government reports that the need for real-time information spawned yet another task force: the Real-Time Tools Best Practices Task Force, assembled to identify best practices for building and maintaining real-time networks in the energy industry. Real-time information clearly has an important role to play in power network maintenance; predictive techniques might have prevented the massive 2003 power outage and would assuredly reduce the risk of a recurrence.

Ironically, the vulnerability of the power grid and potential for social and economic disruption that could be caused by a major power outage had previously been identified as one of several "cyber threats" by the 1998 Presidential Commission on Critical Infrastructure Protection. The commission found that simple flaws could be created by terrorists and masked as latent system problems, and then be exploited at a critical time to cause a large-scale failure. To mitigate this risk, and upon the recommendation of the commission, President Bill Clinton mandated a wide range of security measures applying to all aspects of infrastructure, including the use of real-time sensors and active management of the power grid.[5]

Research quantifies the cost of blackouts—and the cost of real-time monitoring—as follows: "If the existing 157,000 miles of transmission lines in the United States were fitted with $25,000 sensors every 10 miles, and each sensor were replaced every five years, the annual cost would be $100 million. This would increase the average residential electricity bill (now $.10 per kilowatt-hour) to 10.004 cents per kilowatt-hour. The total would be roughly one-tenth the estimated annual cost of blackouts."[6]

The North American Energy Reliability Council is working on standards for implementing these protections across the na-

5 DAY INLAND

TUE	WED	THU	FRI	SAT
76	70	66	60	61
55	50	48	35	33

Variable Demand for Energy Resources. Demand and consumption can change rapidly and significantly. A city's power consumption might be low and consistent for months, but a change in weather conditions will spike demand. If unidentified and unbalanced, lack of energy resources can lead to poor customer satisfaction and potentially dangerous situations.

tional power grid. The goal is to create a real-time sensor network with predictive monitoring, analysis and response that could keep electricity flowing regardless of transmission line failures or even terrorist attacks.

PEAK OIL

Few predictions draw more attention these days than attempts to pinpoint when the world will begin to run out of oil. "Peak oil," as it is known, is the time that production will begin to diminish. Some say that a crisis is imminent. However, the latest analysis from Cambridge Energy Research Associates (CERA), a prominent energy consultant, points to increased production over the next few years and a peak in the third or fourth decade of this century. Actually, the researchers say it will be an "undulating plateau" rather than a peak and will continue for several decades.[7]

These predictions are comforting. Yet CERA researchers point out, "The main risks to our Supply Expansion scenario are above ground, not below ground—changes in the political and operating climate that could delay expansion."[8] Unfortunately, these above-ground risks are very real and they have sent oil prices soaring to record highs.

The rising price of oil has led to increased efforts to maximize the production of every oil well and field, large and small. The U.S. Department of Energy's National Energy Technology Laboratory, for example, has developed an "ultra-cost" method for monitoring marginal oil wells that promises to help rescue thousands of wells from an early demise.

At least 75 percent of U.S. oil wells are "stripper wells," producing less than 15 barrels daily. Despite their low volumes, these wells account for a combined potential production of nearly a million barrels a day. Most have, however, operated at marginal profit until recently. Between 1993 and 2000 (when oil prices were lower than now), about 150,000 of these marginal oil wells were abandoned for economic reasons.[9]

Today there is growing interest in reopening these wells but each must be proven capable of producing enough oil to make operations viable. The Marginal Expense Oilwell Wireless Surveillance (MEOWS) monitoring system, developed by the National Energy Technology Laboratory, addresses this need.

MEOWS enables remote monitoring of wells in real time at significantly reduced cost, as compared to the systems used at high-production wells such as those in the Gulf of Mexico. The low-cost systems use wireless-enabled vibration sensors attached to a well's flow-line check valves to determine oil flow conditions.

Collecting the data is, of course, just the beginning. Real-time and historical data are then used to predict when an oil well will peak and drive decisions on when it is no longer viable.

DIGITAL OIL FIELD OF THE FUTURE

MEOWS is a small subset of a much grander vision that is widely discussed throughout the oil industry and beginning to be implemented in trials. Variously known as the digital oil field of the future (DOFF) or x-field, it involves the application of leading-edge technologies to oil production and distribution operations.

"Oil and gas producers are looking to integrate global operations and the energy supply chain into a cohesive picture including exploration and production, distribution, marketing and sales, even trading, financial and fiscal and environmental reporting activities," says Andy Howell of Aspen Technology, a leader in process engineering in the oil and gas industry.[10]

Real-time data plays a central role in this vision. "Identifying and assembling the correct, complete information, in the right context, often from disparate sources and across multiple operating companies is the challenge," writes Paul Helm of Hewlett-Packard. He continues, "Informed decisions on the viability of aging assets, remote support for realtime drilling operations, realtime visibility of produced oil in water for environmental compliance or the optimized staging of spares in field support operations all require access to current 'realtime' information."[11]

DOFF is aimed at boosting the production of oil fields while reducing costs. CERA has reported, for example, that the use of advanced digital technologies could potentially increase world oil reserves by 125 billion barrels, an amount greater than either Iraq's current reserves or the combined reserves of Latin American countries.[12]

At the heart of DOFF is a shift from the use of historical data alone to real-time data collection and analysis. This transition enables operators to visualize what is happening underground and predict what needs to happen to maximize production and efficiently manage an oil field.

Already, many oil producers are using real-time data collected during drilling operations to steer the path of the well and maximize production. Sensors installed in wells also enable operators to spot and avoid potential problems. The next big wave of DOFF, Howell says, will involve predicting potential problems in wells and pipelines before they occur. "In the future full, closed loop, advanced process control systems will self-tune production systems so that automatic and predictive operation of the production equipment will yield the elusive 100 percent uptime record."[13]

The oil and gas industries, more than most, have recognized the value of predictive technologies. Industry leaders appear set to take the plunge into the world of DOFF. There is too much at stake—as the volatility of oil prices and supplies rock the global economy—for them not to do so.

The Proactive Oil Field. The real-time information network helps management see a declining production level trend at Well #5. By correlating the production challenges with the available staff and opportunity cost trade-off, management can direct a sub-set of staff to help identify and remedy the problem.

OIL TRADING

Crude oil production and distribution present two of the world's most complicated supply chain challenges, largely due to the complexities of oil transportation and the number of agents involved in producing and marketing petroleum. Brokers can track up to 350 grades of crude oil produced by more than 850 refineries around the world. They deal with a myriad of companies handling production, pipelines, financing, tariffs and many other variables.

The data systems used by oil traders, like those in many other commodity markets, must provide real-time information. However, they must also incorporate several sources of critical data, ranging from the real-time price information of the futures exchanges to ship position reports and wire-service news bulletins, all in differing formats.

Combining these data sources to create a real-time information feed for oil traders was the challenge faced by OILspace, a leading provider of data services to the oil industry.

OILspace created an online portal that allows customers to access relevant data quickly. OILspace also allows brokers to publish information directly to the portal, enabling two-way communication with key markets. Users can access relevant data online, analyze current and historical data, collaborate with colleagues and partners—even access market data through wireless devices.

ENERGY TRADING

If we were to turn back the clock by a few years, energy trading would be the major focus of this chapter. From the mid-1990s through 2001, online energy trading flourished as American states deregulated electricity and gas to create an open market. Trading floors were outfitted with the latest real-time information systems, by the dozen. In 1999, a new Web-based trading operation called Enron Online was born. Two years later, Enron Online was making 6,000 trades a day, with average daily revenue of $2.5 billion. All of these trades were facilitated electronically.[14] Energy trading went international in 2000 with the launch of the InterContinental Exchange (ICE), which also grew rapidly and went on to acquire London's International Petroleum Exchange, the home of oil futures trading.

The first signs of trouble came when California declared an energy emergency in January 2001. The state had to bail out Pacific Gas & Electric and other deregulated utilities that had purchased wholesale contracts at massively inflated prices but could not pass the costs on to consumers. Blackouts and brownouts became commonplace in one of the most populous states of the union. It was, in short, a disaster.

Then came the Enron scandal. "Trading shrank, alongside credit rating downgrades, a loss of confidence and the hurried departure of U.S. power trading companies from Europe," wrote Anne Ku, an energy industry reporter.[15]

It was not only the energy trading sector that felt the effects. New accounting regulations and the Sarbanes-Oxley Act were introduced to ensure that publicly traded companies could not conduct sham trades or hide trading losses, while forcing companies to make their financial reports more transparent and holding top executives personally responsible for the accuracy of those reports. As Enron's executives were brought to justice, the term "perp walk" (the police action of parading an arrested suspect in handcuffs before the media) entered the common lexicon. Simultaneously, "energy trading" took on a shady reputation, and many of the companies that had been active in the market withdrew or scaled down their involvement.

After these events it is fair to ask whether real-time trading systems enabled fraud. The answer, of course, is that almost any technology can be abused, whether it is the e-mail system that enables spam or the high-speed car that provides a fast getaway for bank robbers. In this instance, yes, real-time data technology was abused. The old adage "garbage in, garbage out" comes to mind. Real time simply accelerated that process! This does not negate the value of real-time data or predictive technologies. Rather, it should serve as a warning that a real-time environment alone cannot ensure fair trading. Market regulation is essential, whether imposed by authorities or adopted voluntarily by market participants. A predictive compliance solution could prevent future abuses such as those found in the Enron case but only if the rules are in place to define how the market is supposed to operate.

PREDICTIVE BUSINESS IN ENERGY UTILITIES

Some might link Enron's ability to perpetrate the level of fraud that resulted in its collapse to the deregulation of electricity markets. Certainly, many residents of California who suffered through widespread power outages and brownouts in 2001 and 2002 place the blame on deregulation, and this discouraged several other states from moving in the same direction.

Yet over time, energy utilities that once operated on a regional basis will compete on the world stage. In Europe, the markets are

Essent Energie in the Hot Seat

Deregulation ranks at the top of the list of disruptive business events. As we have seen in the United States, deregulation can force the breakup of one of the world's most highly respected companies, AT&T. It can also create circumstances that lead to the most infamous of business scandals, at Enron.

While companies facing deregulation must deal with massive upheaval, they typically have some time to consider the consequences of resisting or embracing change.

Essent Energie, the vertically integrated Dutch utilities group, took the latter course when it faced the prospect of market deregulation in 2002. While fighting its cause on the political front, the company moved to transform itself into a customer-friendly, flexible and adaptable enterprise.

In advance of deregulation, Essent upgraded its IT systems by deploying best-in-class applications such as SAP and Siebel. Yet the company quickly recognized that these stand-alone applications were not enough. Although new software applications had made various operations more efficient, they did not provide the real-time information flow that would be critical when market barriers were removed. Essent needed a comprehensive integration framework tying all of its systems together.

Essent's challenge was to win and hold on to customers who would suddenly have a lot more choices in their purchases of gas and electricity. The company, which had previously focused on the B2B market, was also moving into the consumer sector.

Improving customer service drove the integration project, but there were multiple complex issues to resolve. Essent's situation was complicated by the way in which business processes are completed. For example, quotations have to be sent to a pricing desk, which in turn sends out a requisition for the quotation. The quote must take into consideration the customer's usage profile, which is also needed for metering purposes. The set of interlinked processes was slow; the company needed real-time information to provide superior customer service.

In addition, the company wanted to collect metering data from multiple sources so that it would be able to effectively monitor and manage power consumption. These requirements are common among energy companies but the company had no prior experience dealing with these issues. Finally, Essent Energie wanted a solution that would allow for expansion of its retail operations and provide access to information for cross- and up-selling opportunities.

Frans Schoot, Essent's manager of information management systems, noted, "We wanted a solution that is open and not dependent on certain server technology; we needed flexibility because we are going through a period of change and this is when reliability problems occur."[1] But there were other constraints. "We had to have everything ready to go for 1st April 2002 because of the new market conditions; we knew that speed to completion would give us an enormous advantage—we're the only ones to have achieved that."[2]

But that was not the end of the story. As this book is being written, Essent Energie faces the next phase of Dutch energy market deregulation, which may force a breakup of the company's energy generation and distribution operations. Meanwhile, smaller Dutch energy companies are being swallowed up by larger European utilities companies in a binge of acquisitions. The Dutch energy market is now, to put it bluntly, in play.

Essent's bold moves to transform itself from a sleepy government-regulated company into a competitive, customer-centric, real-time energy industry leader will maximize its opportunities in this turbulent period. Whether these will be enough to protect it from the "perfect business storm" is—dare I say it—impossible to predict.

already being opened up to industrial users; by 2007, it will be possible for European citizens to choose from any European supplier.

This will add to the complexities of buying and selling energy services. Will it also mean the introduction of a fresh wave of price volatility? No one knows, but governments will undoubtedly intervene to protect consumers.

Nevertheless, energy companies will need to ensure their ability to predict supply, demand and pricing. This will undoubtedly lead to further integration as the global energy industry becomes more like the global financial markets. In that sense, the revolution we saw on Wall Street that started in the 1980s (when trading operations were digitized) will be increasingly reflected among global energy traders. It's already happening. As companies strive to meet customer demand at the best possible price while mitigating risk factors, they are constructing comprehensive long- and short-term plans designed to optimize their energy portfolios. The next step is real-time event analysis. Then the results can be applied to reduce the financial exposure that results from maintaining a margin of safety—at times of peak load, when there is an excess of supply or where risks to service disruption arise.

Researchers in California, for example, have demonstrated a workable real-time Demand Response Business Network (DRBiz-Net), a statewide business-to-business network for power demand reductions during periods of peak usage. Wide-scale adoption of DRBizNet architecture will facilitate an efficient electronic collaboration and transparent exchange of information between business entities in the California energy market.

The second phase of this DRBizNet project is aimed at creating a multistate demonstration of a predictive demand remediation system involving California Independent Service Operator,

Pacific Gas & Electric Company, Southern California Edison, Silicon Valley Power, two out-of-state providers and Utility Integration Solutions Inc.. The automated system will negotiate with suppliers and commercial consumers the cost of removing or reducing demand during times of critical power availability. The system will respond to changes in supply using a network of real-time sensors, effectively resolving each crisis before it becomes one. This begins to demonstrate the value of the Predictive Power Grid.

chapter

THE PREDICTIVE
BATTLESPACE

ALTHOUGH DEFENSE IS often perceived as being on the bleeding edge of technology, the reality is rather different. In contrast to many other business segments, defense has been relatively slow to adapt to technological change. This is largely because the defense and security services are characterized by caution and conservatism. Military leaders are naturally skeptical about technology's ability to meet the problems associated with uncertainty—the so-called "fog of war"—which have bedeviled military leaders for centuries. Many argue the nature of war is so uncertain that no amount of technology can make a demonstrable difference to outcomes. I fundamentally disagree with this view. It is defeatist and rooted in a different reality from the one I see unfolding.

FROM THERE TO HERE

During the Cold War era, threats were typically countered by first confirming suspected threats and then building military platforms and weapons to overcome them. This was a tried and tested way of working. So while tools and tactics evolved, there was little adaptation in areas such as organizational structure, doctrine or strategy, and the result was an ostensibly powerful but cumbersome organization. The Department of Defense (DoD) weapons and strategy production cycle is still as long as 25 years, while a typical commercial cycle is six months to five years.

Organizationally, the four military departments saw themselves as superior to each of their counterparts, and there was considerable rivalry among the different armed services and intelligence units. In his seminal work, *Lifting the Fog of War*, Bill Owens observes that this notion of superiority had become institutionalized to the point where epithets like, "There are only two kinds of ships: submarines and targets," were all too common.[1] Owens argues, among other things, that a revolution was needed to transform the world's largest superpower from a position of relative weakness to one where its perceived military strength is capable of results. Owens' central thesis is that military superiority is achieved by integrating intelligence and precision strike and communications technologies. These elements are wrapped in an approach described as a revolution in military affairs, characterized by network-centric warfare, a term I will explain in detail later. Along with other top military leaders, Owens draws on the commercial experience, particularly in the area of proliferating networks and the commoditization of products, as pointers to the direction of modern defense tactics and strategy.

Today's defense challenges are more complex than ever before. While opponents used to be nation states, they are now just as likely to be loose alliances of terrorists, fighting in ways we cannot understand. Applying technology to improve existing solutions becomes moot. When advanced technology is prolific and relatively cheap, as it is today, technology's focus shifts to gathering and distributing detailed real-time information about the locations, weaponry and activities of all combatants.

An example of this transition is in the arena of unmanned reconnaissance sensors. These provide commanders with information that allows them to consider where humans and machines can be best utilized, but without the potential for casualties during the scouting process. Sensors like these are a criterion for readiness to adopt predictive approaches and technologies. The ultimate objective is to persuade the enemy that the combination of far-reaching, deep and relevant information *alongside* the *threat* of obliteration will force surrender as early as possible. The result should be minimal casualties for both sides in the shortest time.

Given the changing face of warfare, it is now clear that power rests with those who possess the most up-to-date, complete and accurate information. Real-time access and widespread information sharing create a common perspective of the battlespace, enabling quick decisions on the fly. This, by definition, is the domain of the predictive enterprise.

It is not only warfare that is changing. All aspects of defense—from troop supplies, logistics and training to how various branches of the services work together seamlessly in national operations and in coalition environments—can benefit from the same real-time and predictive technologies used in other industries.

WHAT'S CHANGING?

Until recently, each DoD organization had its own compartmentalized structure, operations and processes with very limited ca-

Military Intelligence—Past. Budget, roles and, in some cases, the law kept government intelligence in isolated strategies leading to the potential for devastating results.

pability for intra-organizational communication. This was a reflection of what I term the "industrial age" approach to military activity, combined with the entrenched, siloed structure and rivalries noted by Owens.

There were incompatibilities at every level—message formats, communication systems, video systems, frequencies and bandwidth capacity over long distances, along with differences in the way security levels operate. How to bridge the gap between, say, top-secret systems and secret systems was certainly an issue, as was storing and forwarding messages as troops changed location. There was frequent conflict at the operations level: how do you

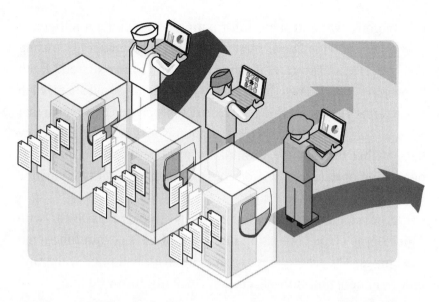

Military Intelligence—Present. Today, parallel systems are in development, and sharing is possible. Yet, momentum is not always unified.

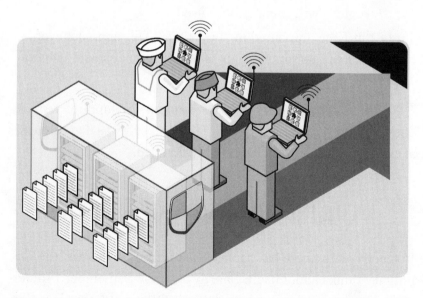

Military Intelligence—Future. Moving to real-time, shared services at the operational level enables a highly synchronous battlespace.

jointly go to war and share information between the intelligence community and the Department of Defense without compromising the integrity and source of the information being shared? Each "stovepipe" had its own data strategy and when it could share, each would only share that which it deemed appropriate. This meant that information was shared more on a remotely assessed need-to-know basis rather than on-the-ground reality. There was no universal publishing of data to a network or real-time availability to anyone with validated authority.

From a logistics perspective, military systems were linear, with rigid supply chains operating in branch-of-service and functional stovepipes. They were reactive, hierarchical, had poor scalability and were consumption-based. They usually followed one of two models:[2]

Mass-Based, with a "days of supply" metric. This model may still be used where demand is stable and where excess inventory will eventually be used.

Just in Time, measured in "flow time." This approach works well but its supply chain is highly inflexible and vulnerable to breakdown.

Inevitably, this meant that vast amounts of supplies were requested, regardless of true needs. The net result was that resources at every level were wasted or simply dumped.

THE INFORMATION AGE MODEL

In recent years, there has been a seismic shift in the way the U.S. military thinks about itself. Shortly after the September 11th terrorist attacks, the DoD established the Office of Force Transformation (OFT). Self-designated a "think and do" tank, its charter is to transform the U.S. military in the following interdependent areas:[3]

How business is conducted within the DoD,

How the DoD conducts business with other agencies, and

How U.S. forces will conduct warfare.

Its initiatives include Network-Centric Warfare (NCW), Sense and Respond Logistics (S&RL) and Operationally Responsive Space.[4] It has conducted workshops on transforming military culture to move from risk-averse to risk-mitigating decisions. Since the time it was established, OFT has identified several key areas for operational improvement. The OFT initiatives described below have moved the U.S. military toward being a real-time enterprise architecture for conflict management. Both NCW and S&RL depend upon the free flow of operational information among organizations. This closely correlates to large commercial ventures that survive on these same levels of shared information. Like large companies prepared for Predictive Business, the U.S. military is ready to move to a predictive battlespace. In this environment, the ubiquitous sensor model of NCW will feed complex event processing and inference-based rules engines to align and allocate all categories of resources before they become constraints on the ability to project force. The Predictive Battlespace also enables the most efficient application of force *before* the enemy is prepared to respond, greatly reducing losses and gaining a new level of operational force effectiveness.

NETWORK-CENTRIC WARFARE

Network-centric warfare describes a framework for military operations with a robust network to link people, weapons, sensors, platforms and decision aids on land, sea and air within a battle-space. This provides the backbone through which information is shared and where collaboration occurs across time and space. NCW also enables quick decision-making at the junior and non-commissioned officer levels. When decisions are delegated down the chain of command along with a shared awareness of the battlespace, smaller, more nimble and dispersed units should outperform larger, contiguous, non-networked forces.[5] Applying theory to practice, though, requires a different way of doing things. In response, NCW has created a set of governing principles that inform commanders how battlespace information is to be disseminated.

At the top of the list is the idea that before engaging in combat, commanders gain a superior position in securing timely, accurate, relevant information. In addition, battlespace conditions and commander intent are translated and shared among all authorized participants to ensure a common understanding.[6] In practice, technology is applied to ensure that the right people get the right information at the right time. A number of benefits accrue from this approach.

First, this leads to a compression in decision-making time lines that should allow commanders to locate an enemy and neutralize it before that same enemy is prepared for battle. Next, low-level forces can operate almost autonomously with shared awareness of the battlespace and command intent, even if they temporarily lose communication with central command, control headquarters or other coordinating authority. When relinked to the network, they can quickly retask should battlespace conditions have changed in the interim.[7]

Network-centric warfare has led to the idea of using dispersed forces to provide non-contiguous coverage. These deliver functional rather than physical control over a given situation, radically changing the battlespace.[8] Rather than deploy large units that only have access to delayed, inaccurate, or incomplete information, commanders can deploy small teams of multidisciplinary forces that are well informed and able to act as a single, interdependent, collaborative unit. By eliminating compartmentalization between services and processes, and using real-time data for rapid response to changing battlespace conditions, the U.S. military is paving the way for faster, more effective outcomes.

NCW IN ACTION

There has been criticism of NCW; some believe the nature of current threats renders it ineffective. But the DoD and its top leadership appear determined to pursue transformational change based on a network-centric model. As of today, each service has incorporated NCW principles into its own operations, signaling a genuine shift from the previous focus on weapons and platforms. There are many examples demonstrating the effectiveness of the NCW approach. For instance, during Operation Enduring Freedom (Afghanistan, 2001 to 2002):[9]

Networked sensors and troops were rapidly retargeted en route to the battlespace.

Satellites connected the command center in Kuwait with similar centers in Uzbekistan and Florida for near-real-time shared awareness of the battlespace.

Unmanned aerial vehicles successfully penetrated terrains that were too challenging for human reconnaissance, providing valuable intelligence to tacticians.

Vice Admiral Arthur K. Cebrowski, now retired and one of the principal proponents of NCW, has said, "The high-speed collaborative planning, the high-speed team building and the quickly pulling together of diverse forces and capabilities is a property of

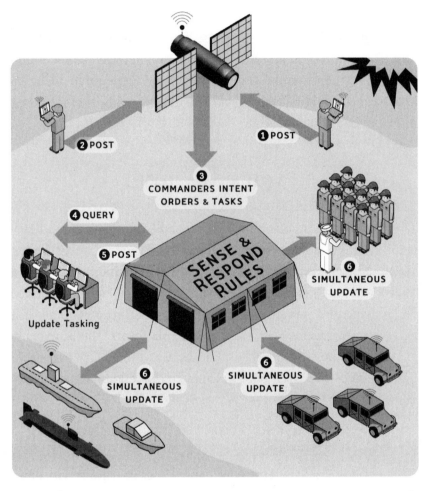

Network-Centric Warfare. Incorporating a sense and respond approach will help deliver a Predictive Battlespace.

an information-age force. So you can see it [transformation]; you can see it right there in front of you."[10]

The Air Force's real-time integrated system for enhanced battlespace awareness, the Constellation C2 Initiative, is based on a model where every platform is a sensor and all data collected is published to a network linking space, sea and ground information systems research, command and control nodes and strike platforms.[11] Horizontal Fusion is one critical element of this battlespace awareness.

Introduced in 2003, Horizontal Fusion is designed to achieve "power to the edge" in the transformed battlespace. It equips war fighters ("edge users") with the ability to receive the real-time information they need through smart-pull and information sharing. It is termed *horizontal* because the system extends across stovepiped organizations, and *fusion* implies its network-centric integration.[12] Horizontal Fusion will be a primary feed for the Predictive Battlespace.

During the 2003 Operation Iraqi Freedom, a number of initiatives were developed and tested for the first time.[13] Principal among these were:

Blue Force Tracking System, which enabled near real-time tracking of coalition troops on ground, air and sea through Global Positioning System (GPS) transmitters. Locations were overlaid on maps of terrain and enemy positions.

Shared awareness of air-to-air missions through secure data links rather than voice communications, which previously compromised security.

Army and Marines could track each other's progress online for more effective operations and quick adjustments. Shared battlespace awareness reduced friendly fire incidents.

Although many of these initiatives were deemed successful, practical challenges cannot be glossed over. For instance, sharing information rapidly and seamlessly with coalition partners who do not have a common base of training, equipment or language represents a significant, ongoing hurdle.[14]

SENSE AND RESPOND LOGISTICS

The supply side of defense has not been ignored. In the past, resources were deployed on the basis of mass requirements rather than according to need. The net result was the twin pariahs of spares shortages coupled with uncontrolled waste at a time when budgets were being held in check or only rising minimally. In response, the DoD developed the concept of Sense and Respond Logistics, founded upon the principles underpinning NCW.

In short, S&RL provides methods that seek to optimize the cost of military engagements while ensuring military success. Today, this means that battle commanders are not only assessed on their military success, but also on their effective use of resources. While this sounds like a contradiction in terms, S&RL provides an end-to-end integrated support system for the joint services that uses advanced business process management principles akin to those found in sophisticated commercial supply chains. It taps into DoD operations to leverage dynamic demand and supply networks, anticipating and coordinating actions and providing alternatives to enhance logistical support. S&RL is event-driven and operates in real time, placing supplies precisely where they are (or will be) needed in battlespaces around the world. So when a squadron of F-15s is suddenly deployed from Turkey to Iraq, all of the associated parts and maintenance supplies go there too. If an emergency need for parts arises in an Asian battlespace, the S&RL network may specify a local Korean manufacturer that can supply the part faster than a traditional replacement order shipped from the United States.

It is important to realize that S&RL complements traditional supply assessment methods as follows: decisions can be made to optimize supply based on an acceptable delay, taking into account preexisting or potential battlespace conditions. It might mean, for example, that certain supplies are not made available until they are factory-ready because the cost of an alternative supply is too high in relation to the operations currently in progress. On the other hand, it might mean flying in supplies regardless of cost because battlefield conditions have (or are likely to) become critical, with the potential for lost ground or increased casualties. An alternative scenario (and one I believe will become increasingly common) arises where a lead unit needs to pause to resupply while support units have no such requirement. In these circumstances, S&RL techniques can be used to inform decisions about switching operational priorities or moving support units into leader positions. Either way, the pause associated with step progress is reduced, further enhancing battlespace superiority.

Some aspects of S&RL were implemented immediately, jump-starting the transformation process, while the rest of the program undergoes further development. For instance, a range of network-centric measures of success—including adaptability, scalability, speed, effects-based, predictive and cognitive—have been put in place.

The way S&RL is being structured draws heavily from the commercial world. It sees every S&RL entity (military, government or commercial) as both a potential consumer and a potential logistics provider. Users are synchronized and able to negotiate commitments through their shared awareness of the situation, desired outcome and command intent. Roles and commitments are dynamic, defined within a specific context and current capabilities.[15]

None of this is possible without integration, and, here, S&RL melds the old operations, intelligence and logistics stovepipes into a seamless support mechanism benefiting all DoD services.

The goals show remarkable similarity to what one expects to see in the commercial world. S&RL is designed to improve force capability and provides more flexibility through anticipatory and responsive support. It changes the way logistics support interacts with operations and intelligence. S&RL also changes the way the DoD interfaces with suppliers, allies and the services by eliminating stovepiped logistics systems that cannot communicate with each other. Supply networks adapt to leverage DoD and partners' resources to rapidly satisfy demand.

There are, however, fundamental differences between what might be termed a business approach and that which works for the military. It has to be taken as fact that, in a military conflict, logistics demand is unpredictable. Therefore, the key metrics for decision makers reflect the ability to adapt to changing circumstances and the speed with which responses are executed. This leads to a different way of looking at the supply chain.

Rather than attempt supply chain optimization, military leaders are looking for superiority that comes from flexibility. In other words, where I have a supply choice, then my battlespace conditions will impact the kinds of supply decisions I make. That might mean accepting a two-day wait for tents while other assets are deployed.

SILVER BULLET?

Everyone agrees that warfare is complex, and some conclude that the multidimensional nature of combat defies prediction. NCW, as it is currently conceived, provides information but does not predict or recommend actions.

However, complexity theory teaches us that the scenarios that typically arise in a battlespace are precisely those that are best suited to an NCW approach, supported by a fresh perspective on the way command and control are organized. Earlier, I referred to the notion of self-synchronizing units that operate from the bottom up rather than from the top down. Because of their inherent agility, complemented by a stream of fresh, relevant intelligence, they are able to bring a dramatic shift in the way operations are conducted. Rather than being focused on a series of single, stepped objectives, such forces are able to compress the time line between series of events. This means the enemy doesn't have the kind of breathing space that typically arises in traditional operations, so the ability to regroup and adjust tactics is severely hampered. According to Cebrowski, "The Observe-Orient-Decide-Act (OODA) Loop appears to disappear, and the enemy is denied the operational pause. Regaining this time and combat power amplifies the effects of speed of command, accelerating the rate of change and leading to lock-out."[16]

But this assumes that each objective can be pursued more or less in line with battle plans. Commanders will no doubt argue this is unrealistic, relying as it does on the notion of perfect knowledge and flawless execution. While I accept that the complexities of modern warfare put such outcomes in doubt, I do believe we are on the cusp of taking NCW a significant step forward and in such a way that Cebrowski's vision moves several steps closer to reality.

PREDICTIVE IN THE BATTLESPACE

Warfare is constantly changing and adapting. Individual acts of terrorism and the potential use of weapons of mass destruction by rogue groups or nation states illustrate two extremes among the threats to security. Exploiting NCW principles can bring an advantage to one adversary over another but not a guaranteed position of superiority.

Although NCW has now become an integral part of the defense discourse, it is at the early stages of delivering a complete solution. Results are promising but they only go so far in providing commanders with the right information to formulate plans that can adapt to the fog of war.

What is needed is a robust analytic capability that provides commanders with a series of scenarios and potential outcomes from which they can choose the most effective set of tactics. This is where the evolving commercial technologies of the Predictive Business will morph like many past innovations to become core to the Predictive Battlespace.

chapter

GETTING YOUR BUSINESS READY FOR PREDICTIVE

B ECOMING A PREDICTIVE BUSINESS is fundamental to the future of any company. I used to say that you are "real-time or you are history." Similarly, in four or five years I believe that it will be true to say that large-scale businesses will be either predictive or historical. Getting a head start on this transformation will give companies a huge competitive advantage over others that fail to orchestrate their analytical and real-time information systems. In this penultimate chapter, I will provide some pointers for those who aim to get ahead of the pack.

Becoming a Predictive Business demands more than fast technology. A Predictive Business is agile. It must proactively and rapidly address signals it receives about opportunities and threats. This requires a new style of leadership, a renewed and closer focus on customers and close collaboration between business and IT managers. This transformation is not an event; it is a process that takes time. Introducing predictive techniques is best done in stages, addressing one or two business processes and then rolling it out through more and more of a company's operations.

LEADERSHIP

While information technology is a vital element of the Predictive Business, all the IT expertise in the world will be wasted if top management is not 100 percent behind the plan. Managers must not only believe in Predictive Business, they must be evangelists within the organization and among business partners, demonstrating its value to obtain buy-in from their top lieutenants.

The CEO needs to be passionate about this. He or she must be a change leader. Signing the checks and giving approval to the CIO is not enough. Becoming predictive is going to change the way your company operates. It is going to change the way employees feel about the company. It may change how goals are measured for every position in the company. You are either with it or against it—there is no middle ground.

Top management support is one of the most critical predictors of success in any large scale IT project. Based on my experience with thousands of customers, I would go so far as to say that without the enthusiastic support of the CEO, the transformation to Predictive Business is doomed to fail.

The leader of the Predictive Business must be a person who can thrive on ambiguity and turn danger into opportunity. It will be somebody who can adapt quickly. Intel president and CEO Andy Grove says sailing a boat requires these same skills:

> The winds shifts on you, but for some reason, maybe because you are down below, you don't even sense that the wind has changed until the boat suddenly heels over. What worked before doesn't work anymore; you need to steer the boat in a different direction quickly before you are in trouble, yet you have to get a feel of the new direction and the strength of the wind before you can hope to right the boat and set a new course. And

the tough part is that it is exactly at times like this that hard definitive actions are required.[1]

There's a restless energy to the leader of a Predictive Business and a dissatisfaction with the status quo. The leader in this type of company will not be concerned about ambiguity or uncertainty. Rather, he or she will be constantly on the lookout for opportunities and problems.

You don't really know what the next fad is going to be. You don't know where the next development in technology will come from or how it will impact your business. And you don't really know where the competition is going to come from or how regulations might change. We live in a world of tremendous ambiguities. The Predictive Business leader accepts this reality and deals with it.

This person is very different from the traditional business leader whose goal was to maintain stability and avoid uncertainty. He (it was usually "he") had employees marching behind him in robotic unison to a lone drummer. The CEO of a Predictive Business is more like the leader of a jazz band. Employees are doing their own thing and improvising. The job of the Predictive Business leader is to make all the organization's efforts come together in harmony.

CUSTOMER FOCUS

The Predictive Business is outward looking. With IT improving the efficiency of many of the internal processes that keep people busy within a corporation, there will be far more energy focused on the customer. You're not going to find a company that is predictive and not focused on the customer. That would be like finding a person who is not physically fit but able to run a four-minute mile. Almost every company, it seems, now claims to be customer-focused but Predictive Business will take this attribute to a new level. Predictive Business is not satisfied simply giving customers what they ask for; it goes a step beyond to understand and anticipate customers' needs. This is essential to the notion of Predictive Business and everything is then driven by that proactive, customer-centric agenda. In terms of how the company is organized, the kind of people who work there, the IT infrastructure—everything will be geared to predicting what customers will want and how to meet those needs.

You have already read about several companies that strive to anticipate customers' needs; Wal-Mart, FedEx and Harrah's are among the leaders. Another illustratation points to the progress by European mobile phone service. Until recently, if you were a mobile phone subscriber using your phone to download a paid service—perhaps a game—and the download was interrupted by an incoming call, there would be no record of your attempt because the transaction was not completed. You were not even identified as a lost call. Using predictive techniques, telcos now identify certain events that typically constitute a transaction. There are certain things that happen at the network level. You connect to the service, you try to download the game. If event monitoring notices a failed transaction, the subscriber is contacted and offered a discount to complete the transaction. This exceeds the customer's expectation and the service garners PR points as well as a potentially lost sale.

ALIGNMENT OF IT AND BUSINESS STRATEGIES

In Predictive Business, IT plays a central, strategic role. Close alignment of IT with business strategy is challenging, but critical.

IT success should not be measured on the basis of technology accomplishments. Instead, success must be measured by the extent to which IT brings value to the business. IT is, in other words, given responsibility coupled with accountability as it relates to corporate strategy.

For some companies this will require a significant change of attitude. Too often IT is viewed as a support function that is a consumer of financial resources. You have a problem and IT is instructed to fix it at the least possible cost. I believe this is a narrow view that doesn't allow IT to flourish as a solutions enabler or add value to the organization.

The role of the chief information officer is usually a strong indicator of whether a company has moved beyond the "IT, fix it" mentality. The good news is that the CIO is increasingly regarded as a vital member of the top management team in high-performance companies. My confidence in this trend is supported by a 2004 survey showing a change is underway in CIO selection criteria. CIOs are now being recruited as leaders of corporate decision-making rather than as functionaries. Their positions in their organizations reflect this. In the survey, 58 percent of the CIOs responding said they report directly to the CEO. Only 15 percent reported to the CFO and 13 percent to the COO.[2]

More importantly, CIOs today spend only 35 percent of their time dealing with technology. The rest of the time they are contributing input as operational executives, acting as business innovators, developing future business plans and performing other critical tasks.[3]

In another survey, 38 percent of the CIOs said they are evaluated primarily on their contributions to business strategy.[4] That may be viewed as a small figure but I believe it marks an important step forward because the difference this group makes will be significant.

Other signs that IT is being more widely recognized as a strategic imperative come from a study conducted by CFO Research Services in collaboration with PricewaterhouseCooper. The study concludes, "Leading finance professionals have begun to recognize that well-managed IT organizations are not just cost centers but valuable business partners that can drive both operating efficiencies and top-line growth."[5]

Convincing other C-level executives and corporate boards to embrace this view and to adopt a more proactive approach to exploiting technology's potential depends on two developments, the researchers said. "First, companies must make sure that their chief technology officer has a full seat at the executive table. Second, finance and IT must work together to become as adept at calculating the value of IT investments as they are at calculating the costs."[6]

BEST PRACTICES

Competing companies frequently purchase the same commercial software applications, so why is it that some appear to gain more competitive advantage than others from their investments in IT? The answer lies in their integration of information and business processes, in making the parts work together more effectively and more efficiently.

Integration is not easy and there are plenty of horror stories out there to prove it. According to the Standish Group, 18 percent of IT projects fail and over 50 percent are over budget, run late or achieve less than the required features and functions.[7] Yet integration is essential. Without it, you have silos of information held in systems that operate independently and won't

The Great IT Debate

Perhaps it goes without saying that predictive enterprises *believe* in the value of information technology. Yet, over the past few years, we heard from more than a few doubting Thomases—CEOs asking questions like, "We keep throwing more and more resources at IT. What are we getting for our money?"

There are reasons for their skepticism. Over the past decade, businesses have spent heavily on enterprise applications without achieving all of the desired benefits.

Despite extraordinary success at selling software, companies such as SAP, Oracle, Siebel, Manugistics, and i2 did not automate or orchestrate every business process. Rather, they addressed departmental or isolated problems one by one. So while individual departments appeared to be more efficient, companies as a whole were not achieving the synergistic or accretive benefits of all business processes operating seamlessly together.

Disenchantment with the value that IT delivers came to a head with the publication of an article titled "IT Doesn't Matter" by Nicholas Carr in the *Harvard Business Review.* Carr's thesis was based on the claim that much of IT is infrastructural, homogenized, and commoditized. He drew parallels between IT and American railroad networks and electricity grids, noting, "IT is, first of all, a transport mechanism—it carries digital information just as railroads carry goods and power grids carry electricity. And like any transport mechanism, it is far more valuable when shared than when used in isolation."[1]

Carr went on to argue, "There is good reason to believe that companies' existing IT capabilities are largely sufficient for their needs and, hence, that the recent and widespread sluggishness in IT demand is as much a structural as a cyclical phenomenon."[2]

Not surprisingly, Carr's article triggered hot debate. *Fortune* magazine's David Kirkpatrick retaliated, "To say IT doesn't matter is tantamount to saying that companies have enough information about their operations, customers, and employees. I've never heard

a company make such a claim."[3] Kirkpatrick cited Rob Carter, CIO
of FedEx, who was stunned that anyone thought tech didn't matter. "Everything strategic in the company has IT inputs into it," he
told Kirkpatrick.[4]

Paul Strassman, who served as CIO of General Foods, Xerox,
and NASA weighed into the debate. In a withering dissection of
Carr's thesis, he charged, "Message transport is *not* the primary reason why organizations deploy IT. Information technology adds
value mainly by improving the management of information intelligence and collaboration among individuals, groups, and organizations. The transport function is essential, but IT's importance as
a conduit is only tertiary. The value is in the message itself, not in
the means of conveyance!"[5] Strassman went on to note that, "People become enormously empowered when aided by information
technologies because these tools magnify their ability to perform
complex tasks. By trivializing information technologies as electronic messengers, Carr would prevent organizations from understanding how to deploy IT in such a way that it can be the weapon
of choice in competitive contests."[6]

On this point, I stand with Strassman. Certainly, getting data to
where it is needed is part of what we do. But that data is also typically processed—sorted, categorized, combined with other data and
presented in a usable format—before it is delivered where and when
it is useful. We are not just trucking data around, as Carr would have
it: we are delivering the right data to the right people, in the right format, at the right times and thus adding value. Carr's transport anal-
ogy may have been accurate in the early days of computing but it
does not stand up today.

The companies that get the most out of their IT investments,
I have observed, look to IT as a way of enabling a differentiated
solution. They ensure that IT and corporate strategy are firmly
aligned, by protecting the attributes, processes and culture that
make them great and by viewing software as providing fresh ways
to approach complex problems. As Carter of FedEx frequently says,
"It's the software, stupid."[7]

provide necessary details to upstream and downstream business processes.

Integration of business applications is the IT equivalent of diplomacy. It requires that people from different disciplines and frequently from different business units work together toward an established goal. On a technical level, integration projects challenge developers to make disparate systems share data. On a human level, experts in one system must be open to working with experts in another; this may involve a generation gap as legacy systems are integrated with newer systems. Business analysts must figure out how to talk to IT experts. Management turf battles must be set aside as business processes are realigned and data that has been owned by one part of an organization is now shared throughout the business. It is also critical that executives actively encourage the integration effort.

The best way to go about this is to form a SWAT team, composed of smart people from each relevant discipline and area of expertise. This is the Integration Competency Center and the idea is that the core of this group will move on to the next integration challenge having learned a great deal from its previous project. "Creating a single organizational body that brings the diverse skill set together helps to create the focus, momentum, critical mass, processes and standards required to build and execute a world-class integration strategy" say Gartner analysts.[8]

Traditionally, companies linked applications in a point-to-point fashion but with more and more applications needing to share data, the result is an integration hairball so complex it is impossible to maintain. This is why enterprise application integration (EAI) has emerged as an essential method of coordinating interaction among enterprise applications. Initially, achieving EAI may increase integration costs but over time it provides significant savings.[9]

From Real-Time to Predictive

At TIBCO we like to say that we "drink our own champagne." By this we mean that we use our own technology to run the business— not only to gain the value of that technology for ourselves, but also to ensure that we have first-hand experience of being a TIBCO customer, albeit an inside customer. This gives us a much better understanding of the challenges our customers face as they move to become Predictive Businesses, as well as the advantages that they can gain.

Our internal progress toward becoming a Predictive Business began in 2001 when, like many companies, we adopted a best-of-breed approach to enterprise software. We replaced custom-built applications with PeopleSoft for human resource information systems, Siebel for customer relationship management, Salesforce.com for sales force automation, and Oracle for enterprise resource planning, among others. And we began using our own solutions to integrate these applications so that we could realize the benefits of real-time data sharing across the enterprise and beyond.

The first step toward Predictive Business was to create an enterprise application infrastructure (EAI). The second was the automation of business processes. And the third was the development of a data warehouse. With those elements in place it became possible to implement real-time and predictive methodologies.

Next the company implemented TIBCO's business activity monitoring software to optimize customer support activities, while the TIBCO enterprise portal solution was used to build an employee resource called "insideTIBCO."

Our initial goals were to make new employee setups more efficient, streamline order fulfillment and enable better customer relationship management.

When new employees were hired, information about them was entered into the PeopleSoft system. Previously it would take as long as two weeks for that information to trickle into other systems. In the meantime, new workers were unable to access information they needed to do their jobs. Now that we have integrated our core systems—using our own technology—new employees get almost instantaneous access to information and services.

Within seconds of entering the new-hire information in PeopleSoft, it appears in Oracle. A return-on-investment study we conducted showed that our increased efficiency in this area saves us approximately $1,500 per new hire. We have also used our business process management solution to automate the allocation of equipment to employees, so new staff get security badges, computers and office equipment much more quickly.

Order fulfillment was also upgraded to replace a cumbersome series of manual and paper-based steps that had to be performed before customers could download software they had purchased. Now our B2B integration solution instantly transmits orders to our fulfillment partner. In addition to increasing customer satisfaction, this upgrade reduced TIBCO's billing cycles by 15 days.

Customer order information in the Oracle system was not being shared with the Siebel customer support system. As a result, our customer support people were not aware of new orders or customer entitlements. Integrating these two applications enabled real-time transfer of data so that the support representatives always knew which products the customer owned and were able to up-sell services when appropriate. Our ROI study showed that we earned over $2 million in up-sales as well as savings on support in the first year of implementation.

We used our own business activity monitoring (BAM) system to help the customer support group monitor traffic and key performance indicators related to support requests. As service requests come in from our customers, they are monitored in real time. The dashboard system displays key support status, allowing customer support managers to see trends and take action to preempt problems.

The expectations of business managers have changed dramatically from the days when they were satisfied with an end-of-month or end-of-week report, according to Marc Masnik, director of TIBCO IT. He adds, "Today, if the manager can't look at a dashboard to see that there's still a heavier percentage of [customer service] tickets open, or that there is a slowdown in the Asia-Pacific region over the weekends, or any other trend, he is not going to be happy. He wants to be able to predict what's going to happen so that he can reallocate resources and be more efficient."

Providing a business manager with real-time information from the system that directly supports his or her business is not sufficient, Masnik explains. "Our customer service manager is not only looking for information from the Siebel CRM system. He also wants to have a view of the customer's financial status from the ERP [enterprise resource planning] system and if the sales force sees new opportunities to sell to this customer again over the next two quarters, he wants to know that too."

Applications must be integrated so that they share real-time data and provide a 360-degree view of the enterprise, says Masnik. In the customer service department, for example, it becomes possible to see how valuable each customer is to the company so that resources can be allocated appropriately.

Perhaps the most important lesson we have learned through our own use of predictive methodologies is that as soon as business managers become aware of how Predictive Business can benefit them, the old ways of doing business become unacceptable.

"The migration toward Predictive Business happens very quickly once the possibilities become evident to a business owner [the manager of a company operation] and they see how predictive methodologies can impact their business in terms of return on investment, changing the way they do business, improving efficiency and service. Once that happens," Masnik concludes, "demand for predictive capabilities becomes insatiable."

SUPERIOR SUPPLY CHAIN

Predictive Businesses need to be intimately linked to their business partners. They will go to extraordinary lengths to permit their suppliers, distributors and other partners to become part of their ecosystems. Failure to do so would create a gap in the closed loop of information flow that is essential to the Predictive Business model. What is more, sharing real-time data with business partners becomes increasingly important as businesses outsource not only non-core functions—such as payroll or facilities management—but also manufacturing and product development.

As I see it, two generations of technology have already been applied to this challenge. First there was the supply chain, or what I call the "build it and they will come" model. Many of our customers built it only to learn that their customers didn't come, leaving them with huge amounts of unsold inventory. Next came the "demand chain." This was more of a "build it when they come" or just-in-time model. But it was not optimal either because they might come and leave if you did not have a product ready to sell them. In contrast, Predictive Business uses what I referred to earlier as the *eager network*. This model can look at events, anticipate and plan based on what's happening and continually adjust.

In the retail setting, for example, let us suppose that you buy a shirt from Wal-Mart. The sale will automatically trigger a sequence of events that ensures the store's shelves will be replenished. The retailer must be willing to share sales information with the wholesaler so when a certain threshold is reached, the wholesaler can reorder from the manufacturer and alert the shipping company that Wal-Mart needs more shirts (some analysts describe this as a demand-driven supply network).

Center of Excellence. Provides business with a formalized and documented matrix of different groups to create cross-functional processes, which promote a higher level of collaboration and performance management.

Traditionally, companies were reluctant to share too much information with their suppliers for fear of losing the "buyer's advantage." In the era of Predictive Business, it will become vitally important to share information with all business partners. The *open source* philosophy—share to thrive—will rule.

How is this achieved? Once again, integration is an essential component. In this case, we are talking about business-to-business (B2B) integration. The eager network requires close coupling between every party in the supply and distribution chains. In many ways, it is similar to the intracompany integration challenges described above but with the added complexities that come with intercompany relationships and potentially conflicting agendas.

Determining which aspects of your business should be shared with your partners is the first step. You are obviously not going to link your financial or human relations systems to the external network (sometimes called an extranet) but inventory management and order systems may well be linked to your suppliers and sellers. Flexibility is essential. You may want to add a new supplier or drop an existing one. You may create a relationship that represents a new sales channel. Business relationships change over time and the B2B network must change with them. From a technical perspective, adhering to standards is very important as this minimizes incompatibilities between your IT systems and those of your business partners.

Despite the challenges, B2B integration reaps high rewards. It allows you to interact with your trading community more efficiently and cost-effectively by enabling the secure exchange of information over the Internet and streamlining business processes that involve multiple organizations. Companies embracing this approach enjoy 5 percent higher profit margins than competitors, deliver up to 10 percent more accurate orders (which in turn increases customer satisfaction), and decrease cash-to-cash cycle times by 35 percent, according to analysts at AMR Research.[10]

AMR's analysts identified the leaders of demand-driven supply network technologies: Dell Computer, the build-to-order champion, tops AMR's list. Next come Nokia, Procter & Gamble, IBM and Wal-Mart. Filling out the top 10 are Toyota, Johnson & Johnson, Johnson Controls (auto engineering), Tesco (the UK's leading retail grocer) and PepsiCo. The common factor among these leading-edge companies is highly accurate demand forecasting. When events arise that might disrupt performance, these organizations respond quickly. In turn, they average 15 percent less inventory, 17 percent stronger perfect order fulfillment and 35 percent shorter cash-to-cash cycle times than laggards who have yet to upgrade their supply chain systems.[11] "Perfect order fulfilment" means the right product arrives at the right time, in the right place and in perfect condition—no excuses. This is the standard for all 10 top performers.

AMR notes that a 1 percent improvement in demand forecast accuracy can yield a 2 percent improvement in perfect order fulfilment capability. But it doesn't stop there. The analysts computed a 50¢ per share increase in earnings based on a 10 percent improvement in perfect order rating. A gain of 5 percent in perfect order rating correlates with 2.5 percent higher return on assets. And an increase of 3 percent perfect order performance means a 1 percent increase in profit margins.[12] Perfection pays!

BUILDING BLOCKS

On the technology front, there are three fundamental building blocks for the Predictive Business. The first is what tech analysts call an information (or service) bus. This is the central nervous system that ties everything together, collecting information from every part of the company. The second building block is an engine for complex event processing (CEP). It is the brain that figures out, "Given this kind of information, what should I do?" The third building block is business process management (BPM), the muscle that provides the ability to create business processes.

The information collected by the nervous system is kicked up to the second building block, which looks at this cloud of events and starts to anticipate and make real-time decisions or recommendations. The output is then delivered to the muscles, to move things through the business process management layer.

However, before you can put these pieces into place, all of your business applications—customer relationship management, sales force automation, billing, and so on—need to be fully integrated. They need to be connected to the central nervous system. This process of application integration is currently getting a lot of attention from industry analysts and has spawned a rash of acronyms to describe various products and approaches (definitions of these are provided in the glossary). I will examine this more closely but suffice it to say here that application integration is the foundation. Here are a few more critical areas, plus explanations on CEP and BPM.

Event-driven architecture (EDA) is the software architecture or framework that supports real-time information—and therefore Predictive Business—and is event-driven. An event might be a customer support call, somebody walking into your store, a payment being received, the arrival of parts at your factory or the times a machine started or stopped working. EDAs gather more data about more details of business processes than traditional transaction-driven systems.

In an event-driven architecture, any significant event triggers a message that is automatically routed to all relevant systems or people. Thus, a customer support call might trigger a message not only to a customer relationship management system but also to systems that control orders for spare parts, while simultaneously triggering an alert regarding a potential pattern of product failure.

Service-oriented architecture (SOA) is another software architecture that is widely discussed in the context of real time. SOA treats the various applications and information sources used by a business as services that can be accessed via a common interface, regardless of where they are or what kind of software or data is involved.

EDA and SOA are not competing approaches. They are complementary and inclusive of one another since both support business agility and rapid change in applications. These approaches should be coupled in the IT framework for Predictive Business.

Business process management (BPM) is the automation and coordination of the myriad tasks and assets that make up the business processes defining how a company operates. The goal of BPM is to improve an organization's business processes by making them more efficient, more effective and more capable of adapting to an ever-changing environment.

BPM is vital to the Predictive Business because it allows agility. Traditional IT systems are rigid. It takes time and considerable effort to make changes and there are always risks that changes to one system will disrupt another. In contrast, BPM allows business processes to be changed quickly and easily taking an end-to-end approach across all related systems. In terms of the amount of effort involved, there is no comparison between traditional systems and BPM. Software modifications that used to take months can be achieved in hours or days.

Advanced BPM programs incorporate a business rules engine. Business rules describe the operations, definitions and constraints that apply to an organization in achieving its goals. For example, a system might automatically change the prices of some goods if component prices rise or it may specify that no credit check be performed on returning customers.

Business activity monitoring (BAM) is the electronic equivalent of minding the shop.[13] BAM software presents a picture of business activity by monitoring and recording metrics from various sources within an organization's software infrastructure and then aggregating and analyzing this data.

Because it understands the business context of the information it collects, it can translate disparate software events (for example, the creation of sales orders and invoicing) into information about how the business is performing (such as calculating inventory turns or the day's sales outstanding). The goal of BAM is to facilitate better and faster decisions through up-to-the-second information, instead of relying on outdated information collected through periodic polling.

Complex event processing (CEP). As mentioned earlier, an event in the context of Predictive Business is any change that occurs and is captured by your IT systems. CEP is an innovative technology that pulls together real-time information from multiple databases, applications and message-based systems and then analyzes this information to discern patterns and trends that might otherwise go unnoticed. CEP gives companies the ability to identify and anticipate exceptions and opportunities buried in seemingly unrelated events.

CONDUCTING THE ORCHESTRA

- Leadership.
- Customer focus.
- Alignment of IT and business strategies.
- Best practices.

- Eager network.

- Fundamental technology assets

These are the ingredients to enable event descriptions and detection as well as the mindset management techniques required for Predictive Business.

chapter

12

WHAT'S NEXT

IN A 1966 SPEECH in Cape Town, South Africa, Robert F. Kennedy said, "There is a Chinese curse which says, 'May he live in interesting times'. Like it or not, we live in interesting times."[1]

Four decades later, the statement still holds true. This new millennium has already been filled with interesting times. We stand at the brink of vast new opportunities but also of mounting risks, at many levels. As business leaders, we have to come to terms with living in a world of uncertainty; a world in which the rules keep changing—through regulatory compliance, shifting consumer expectations, security threats and the emergence of new international markets and competitors.

In previous chapters, we have described the disruptive effects of deregulation in the public utilities sector, new technologies in the telecommunications industry and the business impact of rising oil prices on the energy sector. We discovered imperatives for the adoption of information technology in health care and the competitive advantages that retailers can gain from sharing real-time data with suppliers. We examined how financial markets use leading-edge technologies and how defense agencies manage real-time battlespace.

The common theme is that organizations in all of these industries have been forced to change the way they operate. Their comfort zones have disappeared.

There is no "business as usual" for companies with customers and employees who have come of age expecting instant access to information and worldwide purchasing power with the click of a mouse button. Many of today's young graduates cannot remember life without a personal computer or wireless phone and the years before the Internet and instant messaging are distant memories. Their expectations of applying technology to business processes are radically different from those of their elders.

Globalization of business operations is another powerful force for change. For some this means the loss of local jobs as companies outsource operations to developing economies. For others it opens big new market opportunities as we are currently seeing with the growth of the Chinese economy.

Predictive Business offers a way to navigate through the challenges and opportunities that lie ahead. It will enable businesses and governments to anticipate changes and act preemptively.

Over the past 20 years, companies and governments that were able to leverage the power of the microprocessor—the engine of modern computing—advanced their businesses and their societies. We have seen this in Asia, where Taiwan, Korea, and Japan, for example, participated in the microprocessor revolution. In Western Europe, Ireland emerged as a high-tech hotbed and transformed its economy. And in the United States we have the Silicon Valley, which thrived on the growth of high-tech industries until the so-called dot-com crash.

In the same way, I believe that those who take advantage of technology to anticipate the next curve in the road will emerge as winners over the next 20 years. The only way to thrive in this world of uncertainty is to figure out how to run your business, or your government, predicatively. You don't have to be able to anticipate what will happen next year or even in the next quarter. Just keeping a half step ahead can create huge advantages.

That half step, or perhaps more, can be achieved with predictive methodologies. Knowing that the customer who complains twice is likely to cancel his or her subscription, and knowing this before the customer is lost, is an opportunity to retain business. Seeing a correlation between consumers who purchase one product and those who also buy another is an up-sell opportunity. Seeing the writing on the wall (or on the computer screen) that signals a power outage or a looming problem on a production line can save the day if you can take preventive measures.

Predictive Business is a state of mind. Some of the most successful business leaders have it. Yet even these visionaries don't have crystal balls. Rather, they are close observers—most of whom have honed this skill over many years—who can spot a pattern or a changing pattern of events and deduce when it signals something of importance.

Let's consider some simple examples:

- A potential customer has been mulling over a $1 million deal for the past three months. Not a week goes by without one or more top executives from this company calling your sales manager with a question or issue related to the potential deal. Then the phone stops ringing. There is no specific evidence to suggest that the deal is going sour. There may be some unrelated interruption of communications. But *you* know that it is time to intervene.

- You take your car in for service every 6,000 miles. Each time the car is serviced you have the oil changed. Typically, the oil level is only marginally below full but this time it is down by a quart. This is not yet a problem, but it signals that preventive maintenance may be needed.

- You have received three inquiries about your products from China over the past month. You have no representation in the Chinese market yet, but these calls signal that this is an opportunity you might pursue more quickly than you had planned.

We can all relate to these examples and we might say that we do not need any fancy IT systems to help us spot such looming opportunities or risks. Yet there are myriad business processes which, if monitored in real time, might similarly prove to have predictive value. The warning sign or pointer toward new opportunities may not come directly from the source you might expect. Complex events relate to one another, but not necessarily directly.

If you look back over a situation that arose in your business—perhaps a late delivery or a customer complaint—you know that there may have been multiple events that combined to cause this problem. Perhaps components were not delivered on time, there was a problem on the production line, a flu bug left your customer service center short-handed and a storm delayed air traffic.

With predictive methodologies, this combination of events would have told you, in advance, that you were at risk of disappointing customers and prompted actions to prevent late delivery or to warn the customer that the delivery could be delayed.

Integrated Predictive Business systems "connect the dots" to provide a picture of the potential consequences of complex events, explains Roy Schulte of the Gartner Group.[2] Collecting real-time information from multiple business systems, correlating that information, comparing it to historical data and then acting upon the results is what Predictive Business is all about.

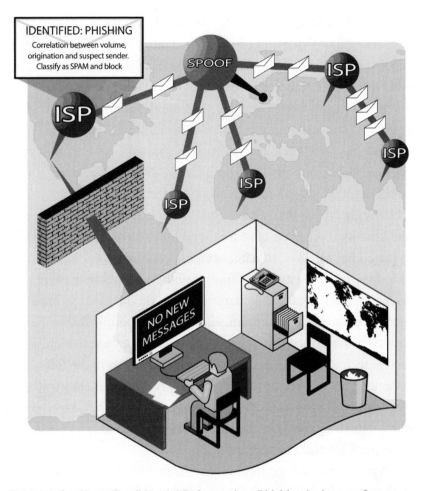

Phishing for Your Confidential Information. Phishing is the act of attempting to fraudulently acquire sensitive information by tricking recipients via e-mail or instant messaging. By seeing the correlation that indicates Phishing such as suspicious origination, a non-trusted IP address with image referrals in the e-mail that are on a "watch list," the ISP can now block the e-mail avoiding un-solicited e-mail, drops in customer satisfaction, and fraud.

Let me hasten to say that predictive methodologies do not and cannot address all of the challenges facing businesses and governments. The wild card is always human nature. Humans act illogically and make mistakes. While we all hope to work with honest, highly motivated individuals, this is not always the case, and while real-time data monitoring can help to identify anomalies that might suggest errors or fraud, to date there are no IT systems that can predict how people will act or respond.

Yet in recent years, we have seen many situations of broad interest and concern that predictive methodologies might have preempted, had they been applied more rigorously. As previously described, the root cause of the massive North American power outage in 2003 was a lack of real-time information. Similarly, as we all struggle with e-mail spam, computer viruses, security breaches and identity theft, predictive methodologies have an important role to play. That role has, to date, been underutilized.

Many of us are already familiar with the alerts that credit card issuers raise if an atypical charge is made on the card, perhaps in a foreign country or for an unusually large amount. Banks have a strong financial incentive to prevent fraud, so they use the latest predictive technologies to assist them in their efforts. In the future, we hope Internet service providers will apply similar methods to root out spam and viruses. If you do not typically respond to e-mails purporting to come from Nigeria, there is a strong possibility that the e-mail solicitation is spam!

Again, I am not saying that Predictive Business technologies will solve *all* business problems, but there are numerous ways in which this approach can reduce risks and create new opportunities. Whether you face equipment failures, breakdowns in customer service or long queues in hospital emergency rooms, it is always better to know *before* the challenge turns into a significant problem.

We began in Chapter 1 with sports analogies, so let me conclude in the same vein. Predictive Business is like Wayne Gretzky racing to where the puck is going to be best placed for his next slap shot, while lesser hockey players aim for where the puck is now, finding themselves out of scoring position by the time they get control. Predictive Business is *not* about foretelling the final score of the game. It's more about taking the best approach to getting that extra goal when the opportunity presents itself.

Similarly, when you take a look at your business, you may need to reevaluate whether the actions you're taking will simply allow you to catch up to the market or place you in a leadership position. You know what revenue you've posted in previous quarters and years (historical data). But, if a retail supervisor reports (real-time data) that the store is having a bad day (event), can you quickly correlate the real-time and historical data to formulate and then implement a new strategy?

Fortunately, you don't have to be a psychic to successfully run your organization. Over time, patterns emerge, and if you can marry those patterns with real-time information, you can get half a step ahead. That is all it takes to win at whatever game you are playing and whatever role you play.

Predictive Business helps executive managers throughout the company in a variety of ways. For example, it signals an alert in the client service area if the customer may be unhappy and about to purchase from a competitor. It also provides up-sell opportunities. The chief information officer is both the provider and a user of predictive techniques, maintaining IT systems that are reliable and flexible while providing actionable alerts if something is going wrong. The chief financial officer can rely upon Predictive Business technologies to ensure compliance with regulations such as Sarbanes-Oxley. The chief operating officer can monitor real-time operations and take actions to avert any interruption.

Businesses that adopt predictive methodologies will be able to raise the bar on service levels, boost the quality of their products and manage risk better and faster than their competitors. Indeed companies that fail to become Predictive Businesses will soon be at risk—of losing their customers, of having their supply chains fall apart, of having their service levels degrade and, worst of all, of not anticipating something that could be potentially detrimental to their business.

We live in interesting times. Rest assured, those who can run a half step ahead will win.

ENDNOTES

Chapter 1. Why Predictive Business Today?

1. Malcolm Gladwell, *The Tipping Point: How Little Things Can Make a Big Difference* (New York: Little, Brown, 2000).

2. Elizabeth Esfahani, "7-Eleven Gets Sophisticated," *Business 2.0*, February 2005, 92.

3. Constance Hays, "What Wal-Mart Knows about Customers' Habits," *New York Times*, November 14, 2004, reprinted with permission on the Teradata Web site, http://www.teradata.com/t/go.aspx/index.html?id=129530 (accessed September 14, 2005).

4. Hugh Courtney, *20/20 Foresight: Crafting Strategy in an Uncertain World* (Boston: Harvard Business School Press, 2001), 4.

5. Kenneth G. McGee, *Heads Up: How to Anticipate Business Surprises and Seize Opportunities First* (Boston: Harvard Business School Press, 2004).

6. Cisco Systems, "Cisco Systems Reports Third Quarter Earnings," news release, May 8, 2001, http://newsroom.cisco.com/dlls/fin_050801.html.

7. Gary Hamel and C. K. Prahalad "Strategic Intent," *Harvard Business Review*, May 1989, 15.

Chapter 2. The Success of the Real-Time Business

DBS Bank's Growing Services Sidebar

1. TIBCO Case Study, DBS Bank, May 2004.

Pirelli Reduces Supply Chain Risk Sidebar

1. TIBCO Case Study, Pirelli, August 2003.

Chapter 3. The Power to Predict

1. Ian Stewart, *Does God Play Dice? The Mathematics of Chaos* (Cambridge, MA, and Oxford, UK: Blackwell Publishers, 1990), 141.

2. Kenneth G. McGee, *Heads Up: How to Anticipate Business Surprises and Seize Opportunities First* (Boston: Harvard Business School Press, 2004).

3. Patricia Seybold, *Comparative Analysis of Customer-Centric CRM Analytics* (Boston: Patricia Seybold Group, May 2002), foreword.

4. Patricia Seybold, *What's New in the Customer Revolution?* (Boston: Patricia Seybold Group, 2002).

5. See note 3, Chapter 1.

6. Aberdeen Group, *Top Fulfillment Strategies for Midsize Enterprises: How Midsize Companies Succeed with Warehousing and Transportation*, Aberdeen Group Inc. report, December 2004, i.

7. Kevin Reilly, "AMR Research Finds $488 Billion in New Operating Margin Available to U.S. Manufacturers," press release, November 15, 2004.

8. Ibid.

Harrah's Loyal Customers Sidebar

1. Suzette Parmley, "When Its Customers Return, HOUSE WINS," *Philadelphia Inquirer*, April 15, 2005.

2. Harrah's Entertainment Inc., "Harrah's Entertainment Reports Record Second-Quarter Results," news release, August 4, 2005.

3. Harrah's Entertainment Inc., "To Our Shareholders," 2004 annual report.

4. Harrah's Entertainment Inc., "Harrah's Entertainment Second Quarter 2005 Financial Results" (audio file, 62 min., 16 sec.), August 4, 2005, /Media Registerpost.cfm?MediaID=16530&PlayerPref=.

5. Ibid.

6. Harrah's Entertainment Inc., "10-K," 2004 annual report.

7. Harrah's Entertainment Inc., "Financial and Statistical Highlights," 2004 annual report.

Chapter 4. Excellence in Financial Services

1. Sang Lee, *Algorithmic Trading: Hype or Reality?* Aite Group research report, March 28, 2005.

2. Ivy Schmerken, "Data Volume Skyrockets," *Wall Street & Technology*, June 29, 2005.

3. Financial Information Forum, Market Data Capacity Planning Committee, "Revised Bandwidth Projections for 2005 and 2006," August 3, 2005, OPRA Data Recipient Notice, http://www.fif.com/md_capacity (accessed September 12, 2005).

4. Robert Iati, *Data: The Life Blood of the New Electronic Marketplace* (Westborough, MA: The TABB Group, June 2005).

5. Ibid.

6. Liquidnet, "Trade Totals (inception through Q2, 2005)," *News and Stats*, http://liquidnet.com/news/ (accessed September 11, 2005).

7. Ibid.

8. Beverly Hirtle and Christopher Metli, "The Evolution of U.S. Bank Branch Networks: Growth, Consolidation, and Strategy," *Current Issues in Economics and Finance* 10, no. 8 (July 2004), Federal Reserve Bank of New York research, http://www.ny.frb.org/research/current_issues/ci10-8.pdf.

9. Alenka Grealish and Bart Narter, "Branch Boom: Folly or Forethought?" Celent LLC research report, August 8, 2005.

10. Frederick F. Reichheld and W. Earl Sasser Jr., "Zero Defections: Quality Comes to Services," *Harvard Business Review*, September-October 1990 (HBR OnPoint Enhanced Edition published October 1, 2000).

11. Scott Forbes, "Creating Profitable Customer Experiences," *American Banker*, November 2004.

12. Ibid.

Chapter 5. Answering Telco's Call

1. Katrina Bond, Alex Zadvorny and Rupert Wood, "Fixed-Mobile Substitution and VoIP: Forecasts for the Battle for Mass-Market Voice," Analysys research report, June 2005.

2. Industry Analysis and Technology Division, Wireline Competition Bureau, Federal Communications Commission, "Local Telephone Competition: Status as of December 31, 2004," summary statistics, July 2005.

3. Daniel Roth, "Catch Us If You Can," *Fortune*, February 9, 2004.

4. John B. Horrigan, and Allen Hepner, "27% of Americans Have Heard of VoIP Telephone Service; 4 Million are Considering Getting It at Home," Pew Internet & American Life Project report, June 2004.

5. SBC Communications Inc., "SBC Communications Announces Launch of Residential VoIP Services," news release, November 16, 2004, http://www.sbc.com/gen/press-room?pid=4800&cdvn=news&newsarticleid=21461 (accessed September 12, 2005).

6. Sprint, "Sprint Announces Arrangement with Comcast to Provide Connectivity Services for Comcast Digital Voice," news release, July 28, 2005, http://www2.sprint.com/mr/news_dtl.do?id=7620 (accessed September 12, 2005).

7. See note 1 above.

8. Niklas Zennström, Skype vision statement, http://skype.com/company/.

9. Sylvia Carr, "Skype's CEO: 'Phone Calls Will Be Free by 2015,' And You Will Text or E-mail 999," *Silcon.com*, May 24, 2005, http://www.silicon.com/research/specialreports/voip/0,3800004467,39130668,00.htm (accessed September 13, 2005).

10. Ibid.

11. U.S. House of Representatives' Energy and Commerce Committee, "Competition in the Communications Marketplace: How Technology Is Changing the Structure of the Industry," prepared testimony of Ivan Seidenberg at committee hearing, March 2, 2005, http://energycommerce.house.gov/108/Hearings/03022005hearing1443/Seidenberg.pdf.

12. See note 11 above, prepared testimony of Michael D. Capellas at committee hearing, March 2, 2005, http://energycommerce.house.gov/108/Hearings/03022005hearing1443/Capellas.pdf.

13. SBC, "The Future of Advanced Communications and Entertainment Services," excerpts from Edward E. Whitacre Jr.'s address at the 2005 International Consumer Electronics Show, January 6, 2005, http://www.sbc.com/gen/press-room?pid=6540.

14. Ibid.

15. Jon Arnold, "The IP Heat Is On," *Telecommunications*, Mid-February 2005 Americas Issue, February 18, 2005, http://www.telecommagazine.com/search/article.asp?Id=AR_441&SearchWord=.

16. Stephanie N. Mehta, "Telcos at a Consumer Electronics Show?" *For-*

tune special report, January 11, 2005, http://www.fortune.com/fortune/technology/articles/0,15114,1016361,00.html.

17. Ryan Kim, "SBC and Comcast Want It All: Telecom Giants in Race to Offer Phone, Net, TV Combo Deal," *San Francisco Chronicle*, July 31, 2005, http://www.sfgate.com/cgi-bin/article.cgi?f=/c/a/2005/07/31/BUGQCDV3BN1 .DTL&hw=SBC+Comcast+want+it+all&sn=001&sc=1000.

Chapter 6. Transportation and Logistics— Improving Delivery

1. Joanne Sedor and Harry Caldwell, "The Freight Story: A National Perspective on Enhancing Freight Transportation," U.S. Department of Transportation, Federal Highway Administration report, November 2002, http:// www.ops.fhwa.dot.gov/freight/freight_analysis/freight_story/freight.pdf (accessed September 16, 2005).

2. Carla Reed, "Global Logistics and Transportation," New Creed research report.

3. The Performance Measurement Group, LLC, "Signals of Performance: Boost the Bottom Line with Supply Chain Best Practices," a benchmarking study, April 2004.

4. See note 2 above.

5. FedEx Corporation, *Fact Sheet*, June 22, 2005, http://fedex.com/us/about/ today/companies/corporation/facts.html?link=4 (accessed September 16, 2005).

6. Fred Moody, "A Conversation with Robert Carter, FedEx Corp. and Sherry Aaholm, FedEx Freight," *Logistics Quarterly*, September 2004.

7. Ibid.

8. Ibid.

9. Annie Counsell, "Doing More Faster and Better," *Financial Times*, February 14, 2005.

10. Southwest Airlines, "Southwest Airlines Reports Second Quarter Earnings of $159 Million; Diluted Earnings Per Share of $.20," quarterly earnings report, July 14, 2005, http://www.southwest.com/investor_relations/fs_quarterly_earnings.html (accessed September 15, 2005).

11. Tony Kontzer, "Wings of Change," *InformationWeek*, March 28, 2005.

12. Ibid.

13. Ibid.

14. Southwest Airlines, *Fact Sheet*, June 7, 2005, http://www.southwest.com/about_swa/press/factsheet.html (accessed September 16, 2005).

15. TIBCO Software Inc., "Southwest Airlines Flies High with Real-Time Flight Data," *Featured Customers, Transportation and Logistics*, http://tibco. com/resources/customers/successstory_southwest.pdf (accessed September 15, 2005).

16. UTi Worldwide Inc., "UTi Worldwide Posts 38% Increase in Net Income on 28% Growth in Net Revenues for Fiscal 2006 Second Quarter—NextLeap Initiatives Continue to Move UTi Toward its Goal of Global Integrated Logistics," news release, September 8, 2005, http://www.go2uti.com/ir/ir_news_release.html (accessed September 16, 2005).

17. Ibid.

18. Ibid.

Chapter 7. Powering Retail and Consumer Goods

1. "Wal-Mart Stores, Inc. At a Glance," Wal-Mart, Inc. news, http://www. walmartstores.com/wmstore/wmstores/HomePage.jsp (accessed September 17, 2005).

2. S. Robson (Rob) Walton, "Symposium: Buyer Power and Antitrust: Wal-Mart, Supplier-Partners, and the Buyer Power Issue," *American Bar Association Antitrust Law Journal,* (2005) 72, no. 2.

3. Ibid.

4. Ibid.

5. Wal-Mart Stores, Inc. Shareholders' Meeting, June 3, 2005 (transcribed by Fair Disclosure Wire, transcript 060305ag.727).

6. "Vendors Armed with Data to Meet Future," *DSN Retailing Today*, October 1999.

7. See note 2 above.

8. Ibid.

9. Mark Roberti, "Wal-Mart Begins RFID Process Changes," *RFID Journal*, February 1, 2005.

10. Lynne Richardson, "Wal-Mart: Benefits Will Be Shared," *Supermarket News*, March 7, 2005.

11. Mike Troy, "Frequency of the Future," *DSN Retailing Today*, February 28, 2005.

12. "Pet Friendly Embraces RFID Technology," *Pet Friendly News*, 2004, http://www.petfriendly.com/corporate/rfid.html (accessed September 20, 2005).

13. AMR Research, Supply Chain Resource Center Web site, "Overview" heading, http://www.amrresearch.com/content/resourcecenter.asp?id=431 (accessed September 20, 2005).

14. Peter Lattman, "Cheapskates," *Forbes*, July 4, 2005.

15. Jeff Bezos, letter to shareholders in Amazon.com 2003 annual report, April 13, 2004, http://media.corporate-ir.net/media_files/irol/97/97664/reports/Annual_Report_2003041304.pdf.

16. ComScore Networks, "Online Holiday Spending Surges Beyond Expectations, Driving E-Commerce to Record Annual Sales of $117 Billion," press release, January 10, 2005.

17. Ibid.

The Amazon.com Phenomenon Sidebar

1. Jeff Bezos, Amazon.com shareholder meeting audio transcript and slide presentation, May 17, 2005, http://phx.corporate-ir.net/phoenix.zhtml?c=97664&p=irol-EventDetails&EventId=1057327.

2. Jeff Bezos, letter to shareholders in Amazon.com 2003 annual report, April 13, 2004, http://media.corporate-ir.net/media_files/irol/97/97664/reports/Annual_Report_2003041304.pdf.

3. See note 1 above.

4. Ibid.

5. Ibid.

6. Ibid.

7. Ibid.

8. Amazon.com, "Amazon.com Announces Record Free Cash Flow Fueled by Lower Prices and Free Shipping for Customers," news release July 26, 2005, http://phx.corporate-ir.net/phoenix.zhtml?c=97664&p=irol-reportsOther.

Gallo—In Right Time Sidebar

1. TIBCO Software Inc., "E. & J. Gallo Uses Robust TIBCO Portal to Cultivate Personalized, Real-Time Information Access," *Featured Customers, Manufacturing*, http://tibco.com/resources/customers/successstory_ejgallo.pdf (accessed September 17, 2005).

Chapter 8. Predictive Business
in Healthcare and Life Science

1. Patricia O'Connell, ed., "President Bush's IT Doctor," online extra in *BusinessWeek*, March 28, 2005, http://www.businessweek.com (accessed March 30, 2005).

2. Patrick Chisolm, "Harnessing Medical IT," *Military Medical Technology*, (August 1, 2004) 8, no. 5.

3. Scott McClellan, "Improving Care and Saving Lives through Health IT," White House press briefing, January 27, 2005.

4. Bob Brewin, "Brailer Promotes EHR," *Government Health IT*, February 17, 2005, http://govhealthit.com/article88029-02-16-05-Web.

5. U.S. Department of Health and Human Services, "Secretary Leavitt Takes News Steps to Advance Health IT," news release, June 6, 2005, http://www.connectingforhealth.nhs.uk/news/131004.

6. National Health Service, "NHS National Programme for Information Technology Implementation Costs," news release, October 13, 2004, http://www.conectingforhealth.nhs.uk/news/131004.

7. National Health Service, *A Guide to the National Program for Information Technology*, brochure, July 2005, http://www.connectingforhealth.nhs.uk/all_images_and_docs/NPfIT%20brochure%20Apr%2005%20final.pdf.

8. Sheldon I. Dorenfest and Associates, Ltd., "Healthcare Information Technology Spending Is Growing Rapidly," news release, February 2004, http://dorenfest.com/pressrelease_Feb2004.pdf (accessed September 25, 2005).

9. Privacy Rights Clearinghouse, *How Private is My Medical Information?* fact sheet, March 1993 (revised February 2004), http://www.privacyrights.org/fs/fs8-med.htm.

10. Timothy J. Mullaney and Arlene Weintraub, "The Digital Hospital," *BusinessWeek*, March 28, 2005.

11. Committee on Quality of Health Care in America, The Institute of Medicine, Linda T. Kohn, Janet M. Corrigan, and Molla S. Donaldson, Eds., *To Err is Human: Building a Safer Health System*, November 1999.

12. U.S. Department of Health and Human Services' Agency for Healthcare Research and Quality, "Medical Errors: The Scope of the Problem," fact sheet, publication no. AHRQ 00-PO37, February 2000, http://www.ahrq.gov/qual/errback.htm (accessed September 21, 2005).

13. See note 5 above.

14. See note 2 above.

15. Michelle Meadows, "Strategies to Reduce Medication Errors," *FDA Consumer*, May–June 2003.

16. Academy of Managed Care Pharmacy Board of Directors, "Electronic Communication of Prescription Information: Revised," position statement, January 2002, http://www.amcp.org/amcp.ark?c=legislative&sc=position&id=6 (accessed September 21, 2005).

17. Healthcare Information and Management Systems Society, "CPOE and Electronic Health Record Systems Reduce Medical Errors with Appropriate Intervention Alerts," news release, May 23, 2005.

18. "MedStar Health: Evolving with the Times," *Information Builders,* (spring/summer 2001) 12, no. 1 .

19. Rick Whiting, "Analytics Move to the Clinic," *Information Week*, March 1, 2004.

20. Brigham and Women's Hospital, Medication Safety, Web site page, http://www.brighamandwomens.org/qualitycare/medication.asp (accessed September 21, 2005).

21. Laura Landro, "The High-Tech Cure: The University of Pittsburgh Medical Center Offers a Sometimes Bumpy Road Map for Other Hospitals Looking to Make a Technological Leap Ahead," *Wall Street Journal*, January 17, 2005.

22. University of Pittsburgh Medical Center News Bureau, "Physicians Embracing Electronic Health Records: Greater Patient Safety and Satisfaction Through Information Technology Initiatives," news release, February 28, 2005, http://newsbureau.upmc.com/Medsurg1/MartichAMA2005.htm (accessed September 21, 2005).

23. Siemens Medical Solutions, "Siemens Health IT Innovations Drive Workflow-Enabled Transformation in Healthcare," news release, February 13, 2005.

24. Ibid.

25. Ibid.

26. Siemens Medical Solutions, "Siemens Continues Support of Community Connectivity Road Show," news release, June 23, 2005.

27. Ibid.

28. Bernie Monegain, "Paper to Go the Way of Smallpox by 2015," *Healthcare IT News* eConnect, January 2005.

29. Philips, "Philips and Atos Origin Announce Expansion of Philips Remote Services Network (RSN)," press release, July 21, 2005.

30. Paul Nunes and Charles Roussel, "Home Healthcare Electronics: Consumers Are Ready, Willing and Able," Accenture Institute for Strategic Change, research study, September 2002.

31. Lucie Draper, "Mobile and Wireless Solutions: Addressing the Needs of Vertical Markets and Uncovering New Opportunities," IDC research study, October 2004.

32. Healthcare Information and Management Systems Society, "Sixteenth Annual HIMSS Leadership Survey sponsored by Superior Consultant Company/ACS Healthcare Solutions" research report, February 14, 2005, 21.

33. Jonathan Collins, "Healthy RFID Rivalry for Hospitals," *RFID Journal*, August 24, 2004, http://www.rfidjournal.com/article/articleview/1094.

34. Syscan, "Syscan, Sybase Team to Provide RFID Based Pathology System," news release, May 4, 2005, http://www.syscan.com/w4/pr_releases.e.htm (accessed September 22, 2005).

35. U.S. Department of Health and Human Services, *Combating Counterfeit Drugs: A Report of the Food and Drug Administration*, February 18, 2004, http://www.fda.gov/oc/initiatives/counterfeit/report02_04.html.

36. "RFID in Healthcare," Datamonitor research brief, reference code: BFTC1095, October 7–8, 2004.

Chapter 9. Increasing the Voltage

1. Gail Russell Chaddock, excerpt from "High-Octane Energy Fight," reprinted with permission from *The Christian Science Monitor* (www.csmonitor.com), June 29, 2005. All rights reserved.

2. Ibid.

3. U.S.-Canada Power System Outage Task Force, "Interim Report on the August 14, 2003 Blackout in the United States and Canada: Causes and Recommendations," November 2003, http://www.electricity.doe.gov/news/blackout.cfm?section=news&level2=blackout.

4. Electricity Staff at Natural Resources Canada and U.S. Department of Energy, "The August 14, 2003 Blackout One Year Later: Actions Taken in the United States and Canada to Reduce Blackout Risk," report to the U.S.-Canada Power System Outage Task Force, August 13, 2004, http://www.electricity.doe.gov/documents/blackout_oneyearlater.pdf.

5. Presidential Decision Directive/NSC-63, http://www.fas.org/irp/offdocs/ pdd/pdd-63.htm, dated May 22, 1998.

6. Jay Apt, Lester B. Lave, Sarosh Talukdar, M. Granger Morgan and Marija Ilic, "Electrical Blackouts: A Systemic Problem," *Issues in Science and Technology,* summer 2004.

7. Robert W. Esser and Peter M. Jackson, "Worldwide Liquids Capacity Outlook to 2010—Tight Supply or Excess of Riches," Cambridge Energy Research Associates research report, June 2005.

8. Ibid.

9. U.S. Department of Energy, "Ultra-low Cost Well Monitoring Could Save Thousands of Marginal Oil Wells," Fossil Energy *Techline*, January 19, 2005, http://www.fe.doe.gov/news/techlines/2005/tl_well_monitoring.html.

10. Andy Howell, *Obtaining Value from Oil & Gas Model Based Asset Management*, May 19, 2004, 4, http://www.aspentech.com/publication_files/GPA_ Dublin_Paper.pdf.

11. Paul Helm, "Oil Field of the Future," *Business Briefing: Exploration and Production: The Oil and Gas Review 2004*, July 2004.

12. Cambridge Energy Research Associates, *Global Oil Trends*, 2004.

13. See note 10 above.

14. Sandy Fielden, "Ten Years of Trading," *Energy Risk*, December 3, 2004.

15. Anne Ku, "Trading with a Small 't'," *Energy Risk*, April 2003.

Essent Energie Sidebar

1. TIBCO Software, Inc., "Essent Energie Improves Customer Service with TIBCO," Featured Customers, Energy, 2003, http://www.tibco.com/resources/ customers/successstory_essent.pdf (accessed July 29, 2005).

2. Ibid.

Chapter 10. The Predictive Battlespace

1. Bill Owens with Ed Offley, *Lifting the Fog of War* (New York: Farrar, Straus, and Giroux, 2000).

2. U.S. Department of Defense, Office of Force Transformation, "Operational Sense and Respond Logistics: Coevolution of an Adaptive Enterprise Capability," concept document (short version), May 6, 2004.

3. U.S. Department of Defense, *Elements of Defense Transformation*, October 2004, 3.

4. "OFT Initiatives," Office of Force Transformation Web site home page, http://www.oft.osd.mil/(accessed September 23, 2005).

5. U.S. Department of Defense, Office of Force Transformation, "The Implementation of Network-Centric Warfare," report, January 5, 2005, i–ii.

6. Ibid., 8.

7. Ibid., 9.

8. Ibid., 9.

9. Ibid., 29.

10. Paul Stone, *Cebrowski Sketches the Face of Transformation*, (American Forces Information Service, December 29, 2003, http://www.defenselink.mil/news/Dec2003/n12292003_200312291.html.

11. See note 5 above, 56.

12. Ibid., 45.

13. Frank Tiboni, Matthew French, "Blue Force Tracking Gains Ground," *Federal Computer Week Online*, March 22, 2004.

14. Ibid.

15. See note 2 above.

16. Arthur K. Cebrowski and John J. Garstka, "Network-centric Warfare: Its Origin and Future," *United States Naval Institute Proceedings* 124, no. 1.

The Great IT Debate Sidebar

1. Nicholas G. Carr, "IT Doesn't Matter," *Harvard Business Review* online enhanced edition with letters to the editor, May/June 2003.

2. Ibid.

3. David Kirkpatrick, "Stupid-Journal Alert: Why HBR's View of Tech Is Dangerous," *Fortune*, May 27, 2003.

4. Ibid.

5. See note 1 above.

6. Ibid.

7. See note 3 above.

Chapter 12. What's Next

1. Robert F. Kennedy, "Day of Affirmation Address," speech, University of CapeTown, South Africa, June 6, 1966.

2. Roy Schulte, "The Roadmap to Predictive Business," executive webinar with Gartner, Smart & Final and TIBCO, July 21, 2004, http://www.tibco.com/mk/2004/wsempredarc.jsp.

GLOSSARY

Agent—A software component that stands in for a user or for another program and prepares and exchanges information or takes action on its behalf.

Aggregation—Manipulation of components or granular information to form a complete sum. To come together, to collect into a mass.

AI (Artificial Intelligence)—The field of computer science that attempts to model human thought onto computer behavior.

API (Application Program Interface)—An interface to access the operating system or other services. The API lets developers create code t interface with a given application or program.

Applet—A small Java program that can be embedded in an HTML page as a sort of miniprogram for animation or computational tasks.

Application Adapters—Software used to connect applications to other applications through a messaging system. Adapters ensure that the external application behaves as if it were native to the messaging environment.

Application Architecture—The structure of components in an application system.

ASP (Application Service Provider)—Online hosting service for business and consumer applications requiring no (or minimal) software installation on your local machine.

Asynchronous Messaging—Participants in an asynchronous messaging system do not have to wait for a response from the recipient, because they can rely on the messaging infrastructure to ensure delivery. This is a vital ingredient in loosely coupled systems such as Web services, because it allows participants to communicate reliably even if one of the parties is temporarily offline, busy, or unobtainable. Asynchronous messaging systems are also vastly more scalable than those that rely on direct connections, such as remote procedure calls.

Authenticator—A data object that authenticates an identity. Data security programs use two kinds of authenticators: certificates and tokens.

Avatar—A digital representation depicted in a virtual reality world or chat room.

B2B (Business-to-Business)—Used to describe transactions where one business sells to another business (rather than directly to consumers).

B2C (Business-to-Consumer)—Used to describe transactions where a business sells directly (or through channels) to the end user/consumer.

Backbone—A high-speed line or series of connections that forms a major pathway within a network.

Back-End System—Software that performs the core functions of the enterprise.

Bandwidth—The maximum amount of data that can be transmitted through a physical network connection, typically measured in bits per second.

Batch Processing—A system that runs a set of commands or tasks automatically without human intervention often on a daily or weekly basis or as system resources become available. Allows completion of a set of tasks as a single group.

Blocking (Synchronous)—If a process executing a blocking synchronous send is "ahead" of the process executing the matching receive, then it will be idle until the receiving process catches up. Similarly, if the sending process is executing a non-blocking synchronous send, the completion test will not succeed until the receiving process catches up. Synchronous mode can therefore be slower than standard mode. Synchronous mode is however a safer method of communication because the communication network can never become overloaded with undeliverable messages.

BPEL—The emerging standard for assembling a set of discrete services into an end-to-end process flow, radically reducing the cost and complexity of process integration initiatives.

BPM (Business Process Management)—It is both a technology and a management concept. As a concept, it is about aligning your business operations and processes with the corporate goals and objectives. As a technology, it is a collection of enabling technologies (often referred to as a *BPM suite*) that integrate and orchestrate the various assets (both human and technology) required to support a business process. These technologies enable organizations to automate, measure, and improve their end-to-end processes.

BPR (Business Process Reengineering)—A consulting strategy that focuses on altering the processes of business for increased efficiencies.

Broadband—A transmission system that multiplexes multiple independent signals onto one cable. In telecommunication technology, any channel having a bandwidth greater than a voice-grade channel (4 kHz). In LAN technology, a coaxial cable on which analog signaling is used.

Business Activity Monitoring—Providing real-time access to critical business performance indicators to improve the speed and effectiveness of business operations.

BusinessActivityMonitoring.com—Online resource for business activity monitoring information and best practices.

Business Intelligence—the collection, analysis and interpretation of historical data.

Business Object—A software object that contains the data and the logic relating to a business abstraction, such as an order, or a software object representing an event of interest to an enterprise, such as a change to an order or stock price.

Business Readiness for SOA—Today, more and more companies understand the need for a Service–Oriented architecture (SOA). Drawn primarily by the promise of interoperability in an increasingly global and heterogeneous business world, SOAs. See also SOA.

Business Service Management—monitoring and management of IT assets through correlation with impacted business processes.

Cash-to-Cash—The cycle time between cash cost outlays for production/development and cash received for products sold.

CDI (Customer Data Integration)—Defining the data and understanding the systems of a record (where is all that data?). Then, acquiring the data, consolidating it and using it.

CICS (Customer Information Control System)—An online

transaction processing program (OLTP) from IBM, combined with the COBOL language. CICS has become one of the most common tools for creating customer transaction systems.

Clicks—When a visitor clicks on a banner ad to go to the advertiser's Web site, it is counted as a click or "click through" by ad buyers and sellers.

COM (Common Object Model)—A software architecture from Microsoft that allows applications to be built from software components.

Complex Event Processing—Enables the information contained in the events flowing through all of the layers of the enterprise IT infrastructure to be matched and applied to patterns helping to understand events in terms of their impact on high-level management goals and business processes, and acted upon in real time.

Cookie—Information placed on a user's hard drive by Web sites to uniquely identify the user across multiple visits, allowing for the evaluation of user activity.

CORBA (Common Object Request Broker Architecture)— A standard programming specification based on OMG (Object Management Group) standards that defines the interface between OMG-compliant objects.

Core Competence—What you or your company, department or group does best.

CPM (Cost Per Mille)—The rate used by Internet sellers and buyers. The CPM is the cost per thousand page views of a given banner ad.

CRM (Customer Relationship Management)—A methodology and software for managing customer relationships. It could include a database for the sales force, executives, and customer service representatives that describes details about customer needs and history and that provides the ability to match these criteria with a company's products and service offerings. Often refers to systems that work with/over the Internet.

Cross-Platform—Any language, software program, application, or device that works on multiple platforms.

CTR (Click Through Rate)—Metric used to define the effectiveness of a banner or key word usage, generally calculated using the ratio of impressions to actual clicks.

DARPA (Defense Advanced Research Project Agency)—Part of the U.S. Department of Defense dedicated to the research and development of military defense systems and responsible for creating DARPAnet in the late 1960s, the precursor of today's Internet.

Dashboard—Presentation of information in a visual manner most often depicted on a computer screen and utilizing charts, icons, graphics and key performance indicators.

Data Cleansing—Also referred to as *data scrubbing*, the act of detecting and removing and/or correcting a database's dirty data (i.e., data that is incorrect, out of date, redundant, incomplete, or formatted incorrectly). The goal of data cleansing is not just to clean up the data in a database but also to bring consistency to different sets of data that have been merged from separate databases.

Data Integration—An integrated platform for data understanding, data quality, data transformation and data delivery across the enterprise.

Data Mining—A term that refers to analyzing data in a database or databases based on patterns and anomalies.

Data Profiling—By identifying data problems before starting a data-driven project, you can drastically reduce the risk of project failure. Data profiling is specifically designed to discover the quality and characteristics of organizational data sources.

Data Quality—Measurement of data accuracy, timing, and completeness.

Data Warehousing—A process by which stored data is extracted from production databases and conventional files and placed in a separate database for analytical purposes.

DBMS (Database Management System)—A set of programs that manage the organization and storage of data, as well as queries of that data by many users. A DBMS can manage security as well.

DCOM (Distributed Component Object Model)—A protocol that enables Microsoft COM-based software components to communicate over a network.

Decrypt—To restore the original content of an encrypted message. Used for e-commerce or security purposes.

Demand-Driven—The opposite of event-driven. A demand-driven architecture performs tasks only when asked to by users or another program.

Digital Signature—Derived data that authenticates a document's or message's content and origin.

Distributed Application—An application in which component programs are distributed across two or more computers on a network.

Distributed System—Data processing in which distributed applications cooperate.

Document Management System—A system that supports the creation and management of electronic documents (e.g., scanned documents). Usually linked to a transaction (e.g., insurance claim) or a business application.

Domain Name—The unique name that identifies an Internet site. Domain names always have two or more parts, separated by dots. A given machine may have more than one domain name, but a given domain name points to only one machine.

EAI (Enterprise Application Integration)—The connection of existing islands of function (applications) into end-to-end flows with minimal impact on those islands.

EBI (Enterprise Business Integration)—The development of business process flows on top of the EAI infrastructure that deal with the entire enterprise as a set of virtual business processes that span multiple physical systems, networks, operating systems and so on.

E (Electronic)-Commerce—Commerce activities conducted through electronic, or digital, means. Generally refers to any commerce conducted over the Internet or private computer networks.

EDA (Event-Driven Architecture)—Refers to any applications that react intelligently to changes in conditions, whether the impending failure of a hard drive or a sudden change in stock price.

EDI (Electronic Data Interchange)—The exchange of data in the form of standardized documents over networks for business use.

EII (Enterprise Information Integration)—A simultaneously old and new idea where data warehouses and data marts create an aggregated view of corporate information residing in disparate systems, giving business users better access to corporate information.

EIP (Enterprise Information Portal)—A portal used to aggregate and organize the content and services of an enterprise, as well as external content for use by its employees, customers, and business partners.

EIS (Executive Information System)—A visualization tool for making the information of the enterprise visible to those who need it.

EJB (Enterprise Java Beans)—A software architecture from Sun that allows distributed applications to be built from software components.

Encryption—A method for securing data to prevent unauthorized access or forgery.

End Point—The destination of a message, denoted by either an inbox name or a subject name.

Enterprise Backbone—For many integration scenarios, it's possible to enable connections between systems and people using standards like HTTP, .NET, and Web services. There are many benefits, however, to augmenting these technologies with a robust enterprise backbone, such as the event-driven or guaranteed delivery of data, the ability to deliver information to very large numbers of recipients or the ability to quickly and easily add or modify senders and receivers of data.

ERP (Enterprise Resource Planning)—A system and application used for planning and accounting for expected resource utilization. Includes shipping, order management, accounting, production, etc.

ESB (Enterprise Service Business)—Used to integrate a wide variety of applications, systems, and data across the domain to reduce IT costs while, at the same time, increasing the efficiency and effectiveness of the IT infrastructure. ESB software provides a standards-based integration platform for IT systems and data using Web services.

ETL (Extract, Transform and Load)—The processes that enable companies to move data from multiple sources, reformat and cleanse it and load it into another database, a data mart or a data warehouse for analysis, or into another operational system to support a business process.

Event—A circumstance that occurs at some moment in time.

Event and Activity Models—An activity model contains a data model (who, what, when, and where) as well as a higher level of abstraction that provides business context, both for structured and unstructured information.

Event Capture—Ability to acquire all or pieces of information pertaining to a real-time event and using the event as context for the data.

Event Detection—A systematic ability to determine that a certain event has occurred or is about to occur.

Event-Driven—Characterizes an information system, infrastructure, or company that responds to events (new or changing information), creating a flow of information throughout the system that accomplishes a desired outcome. For example, if a customer places an order, an event-driven system will carry the fulfillment of that order through the ordering, shipping, accounting, and billing processes.

Firewall—Hardware or software that serves as a buffer between any connected public network and a private network. A firewall uses access lists and other methods to control access to the private network and ensure security.

FTP (File Transfer Protocol)—A software standard for exchanging files between different operating systems.

Gateway—The Common Gateway Interface, or CGI, is a standard for external gateway programs to interface with information servers such as HTTP servers.

GUI (Graphical User Interface)—A program that uses graphics (images, buttons, clickable items, and so on) to present information and application functions to the user. Examples include Microsoft Windows operating system, Web browsers and the Internet.

Hits—The number of times viewers access a particular Web site/ Web page.

Host Integration—The linking of mission-critical applications, data sources, messaging and security systems within a Microsoft .NET services-Oriented architecture (SOA), enabling the re-use of IBM mainframe and midrange data and applications across distributed environments.

HTML (HyperText Markup Language)—A coding language used to create pages on the World Wide Web. HTML files can link to any other documents on the Web and be viewed through a browser.

HTTP (HyperText Transfer Protocol)—The request/response method for posting and accessing HTML files on the Internet. The most important protocol used on the World Wide Web (WWW).

Hub-and-Spoke—A system of concentrators or routers. Providers of transportation services may reduce their average unit costs by bundling flows and channeling them between hubs. The resulting facility locations are interdependent because of the flows between them.

Internet—A global network linking computers of all types on a common underlying protocol called IP (Internet Protocol).

Internet Backbone—High-speed, core networks that carry the Internet's traffic.

Intranet—A private network inside a company or organization that typically uses the same kinds of software you would find on the public Internet (e.g., browsers, HTML, etc.), but that is secured for internal use.

IP (Internet Protocol)—A set of standards for data transmission over the Internet.

IP Address—A unique number that identifies every computer on the Internet.

ISE (Integrated Services Environment [Gartner term])— A Markov decision model used to obtain optimal access policies in an integrated services digital network where voice and data packages compete for the digital transmission facility. Numerical comparisons are made with other commonly used policies.

ISP (Internet Service Provider)—A company that provides individuals and/or businesses with Internet access.

Java—A network-oriented programming language invented by Sun Microsystems that is designed to write programs that can be downloaded to a computer over the Internet for immediate use.

JavaBeans—Component architecture for Java programming, allowing reusable software components to be assembled and contextualized in building applications.

JBI (Java Business Integration) "Pluggable" architecture for integration technology on the Java platform. JBI specifies standard interfaces for integration components such as BPEL, transformation or routing engines to be connected seamlessly into an integration container.

Jini—Sun's extension of the Java program to enable communication between all types of computing devices over a network to allow for easy access to information and services.

JSR 208 (Java Specification Request 208)—A specification that aims to eliminate vendor lock-in by providing a standard container in which components from multiple vendors and various integration technologies can interact.

Keizan Teian—A Japanese term that refers to a continuous upgrade loop process (as found in event-driven systems).

LAN (Local Area Network)—A geographically limited network of computers/systems, usually in one building.

LDAP (Lightweight Directory Access Protocol)—A software protocol for enabling people to locate organizations, individuals, and resources in a network, over the Internet, or on a corporate intranet. LDAP allows you to search for an individual or a resource without knowing its domain name (where it is located).

Legacy System—A term used to refer to older or custom systems that are often costly and difficult to replace and that present challenges when trying to integrate them with newer, more standardized systems in the enterprise.

Load Balancing—A strategy for sending requests to the most available servers within a system to maximize throughput.

Manage by Exception—The process of automating routine tasks so that the majority of a company's business process is handled electronically, allowing humans to focus on where the most risk and reward lie—in the non-routine events. Event-driven systems can identify exceptions, bringing them to the attention of the appropriate individuals so that a company can avoid risky mistakes and take full advantage of opportunities.

MDA (Model-Driven Architecture)—Object Management Group's software design methodology that automatically translates data to/from platform-independent and platform-specific models for interoperability.

MDM (Master Data Management)—A centralized enterprise solution enabling efficient coordination, integration and reconciliation of the dimensions, master data and hierarchies by which all business data is stored, modeled and analyzed.

Message Transformation—A process for transforming the content of a message from one predefined format into another, automatically. Allows for information exchange between diverse applications.

Messaging—The fundamental layer of the event-driven enterprise, messaging is the transport for all information exchanged among applications.

Metadata—Literally, information about data. The "description of the form" that contains the data.

Metadata Management—Classifying and managing information across multiple applications.

Middleware—Software that connects the systems in an enterprise so that they can share data. Allows distributed computing across heterogeneous computing platforms. Central to becoming event-driven.

NAP (Network Access Point)—A connection to the Internet backbone network.

NCW (Network-Centric Warfare)—Department of Defense (DoD) term for characterizing the leverage of real-time information to assist combat personnel with synchronization and central-operations management.

Network—Two or more computers connected so that they can transfer/exchange data.

NMR (Normalized Message Router)—Nuclear magnetic resonance, or NMR as it is abbreviated by scientists, is a phenomenon which occurs when the nuclei of certain atoms are immersed in a static magnetic field and exposed to a second oscillating magnetic field. Some nuclei experience this phenomenon, and others do not, dependent upon whether they possess a property called *spin*.

NSM (Network Systems Management)—The broad subject of managing linked computers, making sure the network is available to users and applications while responding to hardware and software malfunctions.

Object—A self-contained entity that contains both the data and the logic that relates to a specific abstraction as defined by its class.

OLTP (OnLine Transaction Processing)—A program that manages transaction-oriented applications used for data entry and query transactions. OLTPs are used in most industries for online interactions/transactions with customers.

Operational Performance Management—The active management of a set of methods and processes around IT and business implemented to achieve specific goals and objectives.

Orchestration—Managing and coordinating the assembly of component services (either human or application) to create a complete business process.

OS (Operating System)—Software that tells a computer how to perform basic functions such as saving files or accessing external devices attached to the computer.

P2P—See **Peer-to-Peer**.

Page Views—The number of exposures a particular page on the Internet receives. A measure to determine advertising rates and traffic.

Peer-to-Peer—Often abbreviated *P2P*, a type of network in which each workstation has equivalent capabilities and responsibilities. This differs from client/server architectures, in which some computers are dedicated to serving the others. Peer-to-peer networks are generally simpler, but they usually do not offer the same performance under heavy loads.

PGM (Pragmatic General Multicast)—An emerging reliable multicast protocol standard developed by Cisco and TIBCO in collaboration.

Plug and Play—Describes systems, applications, or devices that can be connected and immediately used—no configuration is necessary.

Point-to-Point Message—A message addressed to a single destination.

Poll—To periodically request information from a server, usually to detect if there has been a change to some information on the server. In contrast, in an event-driven architecture, the server would generate an event when such a change occurs, and polling would not be necessary.

Portal—A gateway to a collection of information and online services that provides a single organizational scheme and access point. Portals can be consumer-oriented, as in the case of Yahoo! or Netscape, or targeted to a specific audience, as is the case with an Enterprise Information Portal (EIP) that provides access to external and internal corporate content.

PPP (Point-to-Point Protocol)—The communication protocol generally used over telephone lines for modem connections.

Procedure—A sequence of actions and events that conforms to a specific set of instructions.

Process—A sequence of actions and events that aims to achieve a purpose (usually a business-related purpose like completing an order, or processing a claim). A process may be made up of various subprocesses.

Process Flow Control—A system/logic for capturing the rules of the enterprise that govern how various types of information flow among processes.

Protocol—Formal description of a set of rules and conventions that govern how devices on a network exchange information.

Publish/Subscribe—Refers to technology that can instantly and automatically deliver to everyone in the environment the information that is needed. Publish/subscribe technology is one of the technology cornerstones of the event-driven enterprise, allowing efficient real-time distribution of information over public or private networks (including the Internet).

Pull—Synonymous with request/reply. Receiving information by asking for it rather than having it published automatically to your attention.

Push—Real "push" is publish/subscribe. Information you want (subscribe to) is pushed to you in real time, as it happens.

QoS (Quality of Service)—The idea that messages may have different priorities, guarantees of delivery, security, and so on—that is, different "qualities of service." On the Internet and in other networks, QoS is the notion that these characteristics can be measured, improved and, to some extent, guaranteed in advance. QoS is of particular concern for video and multimedia content.

Real Time—Done/delivered as it happens. Could refer to the instantaneous posting of information about a stock trade, confirmation of a computer order as it is booked, and so on. Immediate.

Reliable Multicast—A protocol that runs on top of standard IP multicast for reliable delivery of multicast packets across a network. (See also **PGM**.)

Request/Reply—Refers to technology where a user/client application obtains information only when it is asked for. For example, to see if a stock quote has changed, a trader in a request/reply paradigm would have to constantly query a database for an update. With event-driven or publish/subscribe infrastructures, that information is automatically sent to the trader (without the trader having to request it) the moment it is updated.

RosettaNet—RosettaNet is named after the Rosetta Stone, which, carved with the same message in three languages, led to the understanding of hieroglyphics. RosettaNet, like the Stone, is breaking language barriers and making history. By establishing a common language, or standard processes for the electronic sharing of business information, RosettaNet opens the lines of communication and a world of opportunities for everyone involved in the supplying and buying of today's technologies.

Router—A network layer device that uses one or more metrics to determine the optimal path along which network traffic should be forwarded. Routers forward packets from one network to another based on network layer information.

RPC (Remote Procedure Call)—A powerful technique for constructing distributed, client server-based applications. It is based on extending the notion of conventional or local procedure calling, so that the called procedure need not exist in the same address space as the calling procedure.

Rules—The various policies and procedures that dictate how an organization conducts business. More specifically, a way of applying variable logic to software or technology. Rules can range from who has access to an application to those supporting organization-wide business processes.

Rules Engine—Software that enables organizations to create and manage their business rules to support the automation and tracking of rules-based decisions.

Scorecards—A representation of activity, events or data for comparison to a scale of performance.

Search Engine—A program that allows you to search by key word for content on the Internet, in databases or in file systems.

Server—A computer or software package whose services are used by users running on other computers. Examples include Web and e-mail servers. Usually implies a point-to-point, request/reply communication.

Service Engines—A family of programmable network devices that are capable of performing stateful flow inspection of IP traffic and controlling that traffic based on configurable rules. The service engine is a purpose-built network device making use of ASIC components and RISC processors to go beyond packet counting and delve deeper into the contents of network traffic. Providing programmable, stateful inspection of bi-direction traffic flows and mapping these flows with user ownership, the service engine platforms provide a real-time classification of network usage. This information provides the basis of the service engine's advanced traffic control and bandwidth shaping functionality.

Service Infrastructure—A framework composed of independent SOA platforms that enable the free flow of business processes, information and services across and between businesses.

Simulation—Building and executing a process or procedure to help users understand the possible outcomes of that process and how changes to it might impact the organization.

SOA (Service-Oriented Architecture)—An architectural style whose goal is to achieve loose coupling among interacting software agents, allowing firms to better align their business needs and IT infrastructure, lower development costs, encourage sharing of services, complete integration faster and build industry best practices.

SOAP—A lightweight protocol for exchange of information in a decentralized, distributed environment. It is an XML-based protocol that consists of three parts: an envelope that defines a framework for describing what is in a message and how to process it, a set of encoding rules for expressing instances of application-defined data types, and a convention for representing remote procedure calls and responses.

SSL (Secure Sockets Layer)—A public security protocol that creates a secure link between two applications, most commonly a Web browser and server.

Streaming—A method for playing video or audio files in real time instead of having to download and play them through another application.

Subject-Based Addressing—A message-addressing technique that uses subject names to denote message destinations, decoupling producers from consumers. Because of subject-based addressing, publish/subscribe is possible. Users can subscribe to the subjects that interest them, and information on that subject is automatically sent to them as it occurs or is updated.

Swimlane—A concept in business process modeling that is represented as a strip or section of a flowchart. That section represents a person, group, application or role, and many times it occurs in cross-functional process charts.

TCM (Trading Community Management)—To help you realize the full benefit of business-to-business connectivity, companies offer comprehensive trading community management services. The services work with you to develop an EDI implementation plan that best meets your goals and time frame. The custom ramp (marketing) programs ensure that your trading partners are aware of the available solutions to meet your request. Involvement in leading trade associations and participation in industry standards and guidelines development ensures you are able to trade electronic documents with all your target trading partners without barriers.

TCP/IP (Transmission Control Protocol/Internet Protocol)—The communications protocols that underlie the Internet. Originally used and developed by the U.S. Department of Defense in the 1970s for the DARPA network. To be on the Internet, your computer must have TCP/IP software.

TIB (the Information Bus)—TIBCO's core technology for creating a real-time information distribution infrastructure, a central, universal conduit to which components and applications can be connected.

TPM (Trading Partner Management)—Multiple languages, time zones and technologies make it more difficult to control information, products, and shipments at various points in a supply chain. TPM is a method of synchronizing business processes across an entire trading partner network, converting a disjointed supply chain into a unified whole—from source to consumption and every point in between.

TQM (Total Quality Management)—A management philosophy geared toward the continuous improvement of quality to meet, exceed and anticipate customer expectations.

Trading Partner Profile—A trading partner is an entity with whom an organization exchanges data electronically. The trading partner may send or receive information electronically. This includes but is not limited to providers and third parties such as clearinghouses, value added network (VAN), billing service, coordination of benefits (COB) provider, software vendors, application development organizations, etc.

UCCNet—A standards organization that provides an Internet-based supply chain management (SCM) data registry service for e-commerce companies and companies that have an e-commerce component. A non-profit subsidiary of the Uniform Code Council (developers of the UPC code), UCCnet provides a global repository where enterprises can register item data and share standardized, synchronized supply chain information.

UDDI— The Universal Description, Discovery, and Integration protocol. Specifications that form the necessary technical foundation for publication and discovery of Web services implementations both within and between enterprises. The UDDI spec TC manages and evolves UDDI specifications, best practices and technical notes.

Unicast—Communication that takes place over a network between a single sender and a single receiver.

URL (Uniform Resource Locator)—The standard method for addressing resources on the World Wide Web.

User Experience—The overall encounter of a portal, Web site, or Internet application. The better the user experience, the more likely a site or application can attract and retain members or repeat visitors.

VAN (Value Added Network)—An application service provider that acts as a go-between among trading partners and processes EDI transactions with security and accountability at a fee per transaction.

Virtual Supply Network—A term that refers to the electronic integration of the supply chain. *Virtual* means that information and services outside the enterprise (those of partners, suppliers, and customers) are integrated with internal content from the enterprise in a single, seamless flow of real-time information, possibly over the Internet.

VPN (Virtual Private Network)—A private data network, which uses the public telecommunication infrastructure but maintains privacy through security procedures, encryption of data and tunneling. Companies use VPNs for both extranets and wide area intranets.

Work Flow Software—A computer program that supports the modeling and execution of work processes that span humans and applications. It is a subset of BPM software and is considered the precursor to the BPM software we have today.

Workstation—A PC or terminal connected to a network.

WS-Addressing—A specification that provides transport-neutral mechanisms to address Web services and messages. Specifically, it defines XML [XML 1.0, XML Namespaces] elements to identify Web service endpoints and to secure end-to-end endpoint identification in messages. It also enables messaging systems to support message transmission through networks that include processing nodes such as endpoint managers, firewalls and gateways in a transport-neutral manner.

WS-Distributed Management—A specification that allows resources to be managed by many managers with one set of instrumentation, providing interoperable base manageability for monitoring and control managers using Web services. WSDM MUWS 1.0 has been defined in two specifications, MUWS Part 1, which defines the base architectural concepts and required components and MUWS Part 2, which defines standard composable support for manageability capabilities.

WSDL—A document written in XML describing a Web service. It specifies the location of the service and the operations (or methods) the service exposes.

WS-Eventing—A standard that enables interoperable publish/subscribe systems.

WS-Notifications—The WS-Notifications family of specifications, although not a part of WSRF, has strong ties to it. It provides a set of standard interfaces to use the notification design pattern with Web services. WS-Notifications is divided into three specifications: WS-Topics, WS-BaseNotification, and WS-Brokered Notification.

WS-Reliable Messaging—Reliable messaging, per se, only provides guaranteed delivery to an endpoint. BTM + RM help provide guaranteed delivery and processing (GDP). That is, you can be assured that your message not only got to the incoming message port, but was correctly processed by the destination business application, and, moreover, that a whole sequence of related messages between business applications was processed correctly.

WS-Topics—First of all, we have *topics*, which are used by the other two specifications in WS-Notifications to present a set of "items of interest for subscription." A service can publish a set of topics that clients can subscribe to, and receive a notification whenever the topic changes. Topics are very versatile, as they even allow us to create *topic trees*, where a topic can have a set of *child topics*. By subscribing to a topic, a client automatically receives notifications from all the descendant topics (without having to manually subscribe to each of them).

World Wide Web (WWW)—The collection of resources that can be accessed using tools such as Gopher, FTP, HTTP and Telnet, allowing files and information to be shared.

XML (eXtensible Markup Language)—A way of representing data and metadata so that they may be easily shared among multiple applications and organizations.

Zero Latency—A term coined by the Gartner Group that is similar to event-driven. In a zero-latency enterprise, as in an event-driven enterprise, there is no delay between when a business event occurs and when the relevant parts of the enterprise are apprised of the event and can respond. Implies real-time infrastructure capabilities.

Index

ABOUT THE AUTHOR

VivekRanadivé is the founder, chairman, and CEO of TIBCO Software Inc., a leading business integration and process management software company that enables real-time business. A frequently cited expert in the media, Ranadivé has been a featured speaker on real-time computing on CNBC and in publications such as *The Economist, Fast Company*, and *Forbes*.